FACTS AT YOUR FINGERTIPS

INTRODUCING PHYSICS
LIGHT AND SOUND

CONTENTS

Published by Brown Bear Books Limited

4877 N. Circulo Bujia
Tucson, AZ 85718
USA
and
First Floor
9-17 St. Albans Place
London N1 ONX
UK
www.brownreference.com

© 2010 The Brown Reference Group Ltd

Library of Congress Cataloging-in-Publication Data

Light and sound / edited by Graham Bateman.
    p. cm. – (Facts at your fingertips)
  Includes index.
  ISBN 978-1-936333-06-6 (library binding)
  1. Light–Juvenile literature. 2. Sound–Juvenile literature. I. Bateman,
Graham. II. Title. III. Series.

QC360.L543 2010
535–dc22

2010015492

ISBN-13 978-1-936333-06-6

Editorial Director: Lindsey Lowe
Project Director: Graham Bateman
Design Manager: David Poole
Designer: Steve McCurdy
Text Editor: Peter Lewis
Indexer: David Bennett
Children's Publisher: Anne O'Daly
Production Director: Alastair Gourlay

Printed in the United States of America

Picture Credits:
Abbreviations: SS=Shutterstock; c=center; t=top; l=left; r=right.
Cover Images
Front: SS: dwphotos Back: SS: zibedik
1 Photos.com; 3 Photos.com; 6-7 SS: Fedorov Oleksiy; 7 Photos.com; 8
Photos.com; 10-11 Photos.com; 11-13 NASA Marshall Space Flight Center
(MASA-MSFC); 19 SS:Ivanagott; 20 SS: Vaclav Volrab; 22 SS: Karl
Naundorf; 24 SS: Andrey Armyagov; 26-27 Wikimedia Commons: Vlastní
Fotografie; 30-31 SS: Dainis Derics; 32-33 Photos.com; 34-35 Wikimedia
Commons: DP76764; 36 Photos.com; 39 Photos.com; 40-41 Photos.com;
42-43 Photos.com; 44-45 Wikimedia Commons: U.S. Navy; 46-47
Photos.com; 49 Photos.com; 50-51 Wikimedia Commons: U.S. Navy; 52 SS:
Jbor; 54 Photos.com; 55 SS: Plamens Art; 56 SS: Yuri Arcurs; 58
Photos.com; 61 Wikimedia Commons: eyeliam.

Artwork © The Brown Reference Group Ltd

Facts at your Fingertips—Introducing Physics describes the processes and practical implications fundamental to the study of physics. Both light and sound are forms of energy that travel in waves. Light is a type of electromagnetic radiation, but unlike other types of electromagnetic radiation, such as radio waves and x-rays, we can see it. Sound waves must have a medium to travel in, usually the air around us, but also through liquids and solids. In this volume we deal with the properties of light, including how it is produced, how it travels, how it is reflected and refracted, color, and how the human eye works. The properties and various methods of producing and recording sound are covered, including its perception by the human ear and production by our vocal apparatus.

Numerous explanatory diagrams and informative photographs, detailed features on related aspects of the topics covered and the main scientists involved in the advancement of physics, and definitions of key "Science Words," all enhance the coverage. "Try This" features outline experiments that can be undertaken as a first step to practical investigations.

PRODUCING LIGHT

Light is a type of radiation—the only type that we can see. It is produced whenever anything gets very hot, for example, in a candle flame or an electric bulb's filament. There are also cold sources of light, such as a fluorescent tube or a firefly.

Flames from a burning fuel such as wax or oil provided people with their earliest sources of light. Candles are made by surrounding a stringlike wick with a cylinder of wax. The heat of the flame melts the wax next to the wick, and the wax burns to produce light. An oil lamp also has a wick that dips into a reservoir of oil such as kerosene. In the candle and the oil lamp, the burning of the fuel is an example of combustion— a chemical reaction in which the fuel combines with oxygen, giving out heat and light in the process.

The first major improvement on wicks came with gas lighting, using flammable coal gas. This gas normally

A firefly—also called a lightning bug—is a type of beetle that produces a flashing light from its abdomen. Different species flash at different rates so that they can recognize one another. The light is produced by a chemical process within the bug's body.

burns with a yellow smoky flame. But by introducing air and adding a mantle, a white light is produced. The mantle is a mesh coated with the oxides of various rare metals, which become incandescent—emitting a bright light—when they are heated by the gas flame.

Light from electricity

The earliest form of electric light was the arc light. Developed by the English scientist Humphry Davy (1778-1829) in 1808, it consists of two carbon rods, called electrodes, with their ends a short distance apart. When the electrodes are connected to a high-voltage supply, a very bright spark (called an arc) forms

---

SCIENCE WORDS

- **Fluorescent bulb:** Also called a fluorescent tube, an electric lamp consisting of a tube containing mercury vapor, with electrodes at each end. Electric current flowing between the electrodes makes the mercury vapor emit ultraviolet light. This strikes the lining of the tube, which is made from phosphor, a substance that gives off bright white light.
- **Incandescence:** The emission of light by an object that is heated to white heat.
- **Incandescent lamp:** An electric bulb that has a filament (usually made of tungsten) in a glass globe containing traces of an inert gas such as argon. The electric current heats the filament to incandescence.

between the electrodes. Modern arc lights, with metal electrodes, are used in movie projectors and searchlights.

When an electric current passes along a piece of thin wire, the wire gets hot. It may get red hot and even white hot before it melts or burns away. In the 1870s, inventors in the United States and Great Britain tried to find ways of making an electric bulb with a filament that would get white hot without it burning away. In 1879, Thomas Alva Edison (1847–1931) in the United States and Joseph Swan (1828–1914) in Britain independently produced incandescent electric bulbs. As a filament they used a thin carbon fiber enclosed in a glass vessel from which all the air had been pumped out. Modern bulbs have a thin piece of tungsten wire as a filament and contain an inert gas— one that does not react chemically—such as argon, rather than a vacuum.

Cold light

Toward the end of the 19th century scientists experimented with passing electricity through gases: metal electrodes carried current to and from a glass tube containing gas at low pressure. Neon gas, for example, produces a bright orange light, as used in advertising signs. Mercury vapor produces a blue-green light. The inside of a modern fluorescent tube is coated with a phosphor, which gives off white light when illuminated by a mercury-vapor light inside it.

In the natural world, some animals and plants produce light. Fireflies (which are actually beetles) and glowworms (beetle larvae) are familiar examples, and there are also some deep-sea fish, such as the angler fish, that emit light to attract their prey in the blackness of the ocean bottom. This type of light production is known as bioluminescence.

ELECTRIC LIGHT

In the arc light, the earliest type of electric light, a high-voltage spark passed between a pair of carbon electrodes. In a modern incandescent bulb, the electric current heats a tungsten filament until it becomes white hot. In a fluorescent tube, the main light comes from a phosphor that glows when illuminated by the blue-green light produced by an electric current flowing through mercury vapor.

Glass tube

Fluorescent tube

Base

Electrode

Phosphor coating inside glass tube

Tungsten filament

Glass

Inert gas

Support wires

Lead-in wire

Fuse

Base

Incandescent bulb

LIGHT AS A FORM OF ENERGY

All forms of energy can be converted into one another. We saw on the previous pages that chemical reactions and electricity can produce light. Here we look at how light can be changed into other forms of energy, thus enabling plants to grow and also producing enough electricity to power, for example, a space probe.

The major source of energy on Earth is light from the Sun. Without it no form of life could survive for long. That is because sunlight provides the energy for photosynthesis, the process by which green plants convert carbon dioxide (from the air) and water (from the soil) into oxygen and foods such as sugars and starches. Animals are either herbivores (plant eaters), or carnivores (i.e. they eat other animals that eat plants). So if there were no sunlight, there would be no plants or animals.

SCIENCE WORDS

- **Electron:** A subatomic particle with a negative electric charge. Electrons surround the nucleus of an atom. They play a key role in electricity, magnetism, and conducting heat.
- **Photoelectric cell:** Also called a photocell, a current-producing device consisting of an element such as silicon that emits electrons when struck by light.
- **Solar panel:** 1. A device consisting of hundreds of photoelectric cells used, for example, to provide the electric power for space probes. 2. A thin tank containing water and painted black. It absorbs the Sun's radiation, which heats the water.

A field of growing corn soaks up the sunshine, using the energy of sunlight to convert carbon dioxide and water into sugar and oxygen. The sugar is stored in the plants, while the oxygen passes into the air.

Light into other energy forms

In photosynthesis, light energy is converted into chemical energy, which is then stored in sugar and other plant tissues. This is a natural, biological process. But the conversion of light into electricity involves some quite advanced physics.

The simplest form of conversion takes place in a photoelectric cell, like the type used to measure light levels in a photographer's light meter. The key to a photoelectric cell is a substance, such as the semi-metallic element silicon, that emits electrons when light shines on it. The electrons are collected and form an electric current. Photoelectric cells are used to turn streetlights on and off automatically (they respond to the amount of daylight) and in burglar alarms.

The current produced by a single photoelectric cell is very small. For larger currents, hundreds of cells are

constructed as panels. Large solar panels of this type are used to power the communications and control systems of space probes.

Solar panels on a roof collect the Sun's light radiation and convert it into electricity for use in the home. In another type of solar panel, the radiation heats water for the home's hot-water system.

Light into heat

Solar panels of a different type can be seen on the roofs of some buildings. They consist of very thin hollow panels containing water, with one of the large surfaces blackened and positioned so that it faces the Sun for most of the day. The blackened surface absorbs solar radiation and heats water that is pumped through the panel. The warmed water may be used in a heating system—it takes less extra energy to heat water that is already warm than to heat cold water.

POWER IN SPACE

The large "paddles" on the Magellan space probe each contained hundreds of photocells. They converted sunlight into electricity to power the probe's electronic systems.

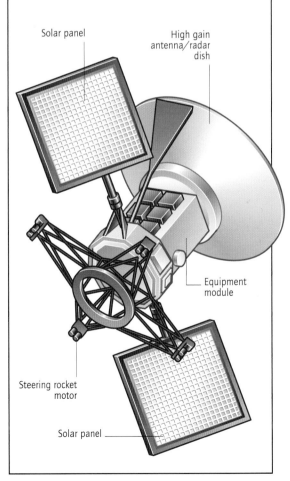

Solar panel

High gain antenna/radar dish

Equipment module

Steering rocket motor

Solar panel

PROPAGATION OF LIGHT

Light from a source such as the Sun or an electric lamp travels out in all directions at an incredibly high speed. It travels in straight lines. Light passes right through transparent substances such as glass and clear plastic. Substances that do not allow light to pass through them are called opaque, and opaque objects cast shadows.

Proving that light travels in straight lines is easy because it makes opaque objects in its way cast shadows. The shadows produced by a small concentrated light source have sharp edges. The shadow is the area that the rays of light from the source cannot reach.

LUNAR AND SOLAR ECLIPSES
(not to scale)

During a solar eclipse (a) the Moon passes between the Earth and the Sun, stopping the Sun's light from reaching the Earth. During a lunar eclipse (b) the Earth blocks light from the Sun so that the light cannot reach the Moon and let it shine.

(a) Solar eclipse

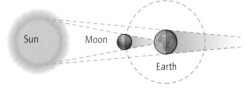

(b) Lunar eclipse

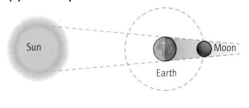

The biggest shadow we can ever see is the shadow of the Earth itself. The Sun makes the Earth cast a long shadow into space, pointing away from the Sun. Occasionally the Moon moves into the Earth's shadow. The Moon shines by reflecting light from the Sun. But when the Earth's shadow falls on the Moon, the Moon ceases to shine. This is called an eclipse of the Moon, or a lunar eclipse.

Sometimes the Moon, moving in its orbit, passes exactly between the Earth and the Sun. A shadow of the Moon tracks across the face of the Earth. For anybody in this shadow, the Moon blocks out the light of the Sun, and it becomes nearly as dark as night. This is called an eclipse of the Sun, or a solar eclipse.

Solar eclipses are important to astronomers because they allow them to study the Sun's outer atmosphere, called the corona, not normally seen because the Sun

In this computer-generated image, the Moon is just about to block out the light of the Sun, causing a solar eclipse.

is so bright. But during an eclipse, the bright disk of the Sun is blocked off, and the corona shows up as a pearly swathe of light surrounding the dark Moon.

The distance between the Sun and the Moon is not always exactly the same. It varies slightly because the Moon's orbit is not perfectly regular. Sometimes the Moon does not completely block out the Sun. (The illustrations on this page are not to scale; the relative distances and sizes are much greater than shown.)

Rays and beams

Light traveling along its straight path is known as a light ray. Later sections of this book explain what happens to rays of light when they are reflected by polished surfaces—mirrors—or when they pass through pieces of glass, such as lenses. A collection or bundle of light rays make up a light beam. Flashlights and searchlights produce beams of light.

SCIENCE WORDS

- **Lens:** A piece of transparent material that, by refraction, changes the direction of light rays passing through it.
- **Lunar eclipse:** An eclipse of the Moon, occurring when the Earth's shadow (cast by the Sun) falls onto the Moon.
- **Solar eclipse:** An eclipse of the Sun, caused by the Moon passing between the Earth and the Sun.

Many of the properties of light can be explained by assuming that light travels as waves. For example, the wave theory explains how light is reflected by a mirror or why the colors of the rainbow appear in a soap bubble.

But in some situations, light behaves as if it is a stream of particles, like a barrage of tiny high-speed bullets from a machine gun. Modern physics can account for both the wave theory and the particle theory of light.

TOTAL, ANNULAR, AND PARTIAL ECLIPSES (not to scale)

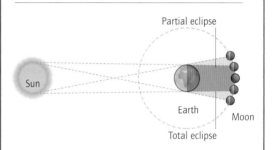

As the Moon orbits the Earth, it passes into the Earth's shadow, making first a partial eclipse and then a total eclipse of the Moon.

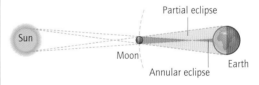

When the Moon is slightly farther away from Earth than usual, it does not completely cover the Sun's disk, and we see an annular eclipse of the Sun.

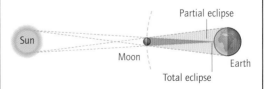

With the Moon at its usual distance from Earth, there is a small region where the solar eclipse is total. Elsewhere it is partial.

SPEED OF LIGHT

Light is the fastest thing in the universe, and nothing can move any faster. It took physicists and astronomers many years to measure the speed of light. This speed is an incredible 186,400 miles per second (300,000 kilometers per second).

When you enter a darkened room and turn on the light switch, the room seems to be flooded with light immediately. In fact, it does take a tiny instant of time for the light to reach your eyes, but light travels so fast it seems to arrive instantly.

The speed of light has been measured as 300,000 kilometers (186,400 miles) per second. At this speed, it takes light reflected from the Moon only just over a second to reach the Earth. Light from the Sun has to travel about 93 million miles (150 million km) to reach the Earth, and yet it does so in just over 8 minutes.

How fast does it travel?

For many years, measuring the speed of light proved to be a great challenge to scientists. The first measurement was made by the Danish astronomer Ole Rømer (1644–1710), who in 1676 roughly estimated the speed of light by observing eclipses of Jupiter's moons. Then in 1690, the Dutch scientist Christiaan Huygens (1629–1695) calculated the speed as just over

Beams of light from a laser show at a disco. Scientists have directed a laser beam at the Moon, from where it was reflected back to Earth by a mirror left by Apollo astronauts. From a knowledge of the speed of light and the time taken for the beam to make the round trip, the Moon's distance can be found very accurately.

230,000 kilometers (143,000 miles) a second (which is lower than the correct value by nearly 25 percent).

More accurate measurements had to await the work of later scientists. In 1849, the French physicist Hippolyte Fizeau (1819–1896) used a rotating toothed wheel to measure the time it took light to make a round trip of 18 kilometers (11.2 miles). His result was within 1 percent of the correct value. Over 30 years later the American scientist Albert Michelson (1852–1931) increased the distance traveled by the light to 70 kilometers (43.5 miles). He used rotating mirrors instead of a toothed wheel and obtained a value for the speed of light that was very close to the modern figure—which, to be precise, is 299,792.5 kilometers per second.

In each method, the rotating wheel or mirror drum acted to interrupt the beam of light. The wheel or

mirrors were rotated by an electric motor. The observer slowly increased the speed of the motor until the light did not flicker. The time taken for the light to make the round trip could then be calculated from the rotation speed of the wheel or mirrors.

Slowing down light

Light travels through air very slightly slower than it travels through a vacuum. Shining a ray of light into a rectangular block of glass slows it down even more. Its speed falls to about 200,000 kilometers (124,000 miles) a second, only two-thirds of the speed of light in vacuum.

The result of the change in speed is to make the light ray alter its direction inside the glass block. This effect is called refraction, and it will be described in detail later in the book. The slowing down is caused by the incoming light waves interacting with electrons in the atoms of the glass. As soon as the light ray leaves the glass block, it returns to its original speed and direction. In this way, pieces of glass can bend light rays. This is how lenses and prisms, used in microscopes, binoculars, and other instruments, work.

SPEED OF LIGHT: FIZEAU'S METHOD

Light is reflected by a semisilvered mirror between the teeth of a fast-rotating wheel to another mirror 5.6 miles (9 km) away. The returning beam passes between the next pair of teeth and then through the semisilvered mirror to the observer. The speed of the wheel is adjusted so that there is no flicker of the light when it travels the 5.6 miles (9 km) and back.

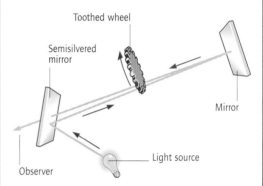

SPEED OF LIGHT: MICHELSON'S METHOD

A mirror on a rotating drum reflects a beam of light to a mirror some 22 miles (35 km) away. The returning beam is reflected into an eyepiece. The image is steady when the drum rotates by one mirror during the round trip.

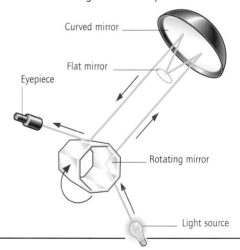

REFLECTION AND REFRACTION OF LIGHT

When a ray of light strikes a flat mirror, it is reflected. It bounces off the mirror at the same angle at which it strikes it, just like a ball bouncing off the ground. Curved mirrors behave differently, depending on whether they are curved inward (concave) or outward (convex). But all types of mirror form images of the objects reflected in them.

All things reflect some of the light that falls on them. If they did not, we would not be able to see them. But the reflected light is scattered in all directions. Flat, or plane, mirrors reflect nearly all of the light that falls on them, and they reflect it in the same direction.

A ray of light striking a mirror is called the incident ray. The angle at which it strikes the mirror, that is, the angle between the incident ray and a right angle to the mirror (called the normal), is known as the angle of incidence. The angle at which the light ray leaves the mirror is the angle of reflection. According to the laws of reflection of light, for a plane mirror the angle of

incidence equals the angle of reflection. Also, the incident ray, the normal, and the reflected ray all lie in the same plane.

Forming images

When a mirror reflects a light ray from an object, it reaches our eyes. We then look back along the direction of the reflected ray and see an image of the object apparently behind the mirror. It is not a real image—you could not put it on a screen located behind the mirror. It is therefore known as a virtual image. An image that can be put on a screen is called a real image.

SCIENCE WORDS

- **Angle of incidence:** The angle between an incident ray and the normal to a mirror or to the surface of a block of transparent material.
- **Angle of reflection:** The angle between the reflected ray and the normal to a mirror.
- **Laws of reflection of light:** 1. The angle of incidence equals the angle of reflection. 2. The incident ray, the normal, and the reflected ray all lie in the same plane.
- **Reflected ray:** A ray of light that is reflected by a mirror.

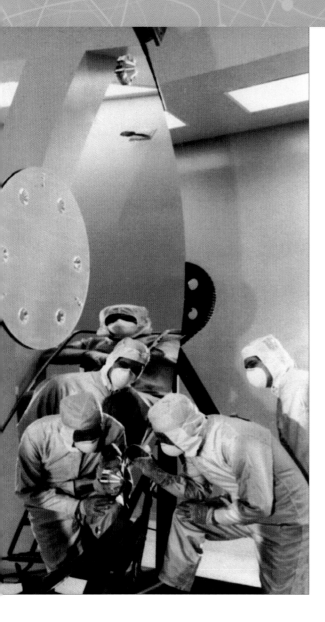

This 7.8-ft (2.4-meter) concave mirror was made for the Hubble Space Telescope, launched into orbit around the Earth by NASA in 1990.

Another property of plane mirrors is that they form same-sized images of objects. The image appears to be the same distance behind the mirror as it actually is in front of the mirror. But if you look at your reflection in a mirror, you will see that it is reversed left to right. Try winking your right eye, and your image winks its left eye. It is as if left and right have been interchanged. Physicists call this effect lateral inversion. But if the mirror is vertical, the reflected image is always the correct way up.

Uses of plane mirrors

The commonest use of plane mirrors is for looking at our own reflection. Every day people use a mirror when combing their hair, when putting on makeup, or when shaving. No store that sells clothes could function without mirrors for the customers. Mirrors are also used to add light and a feeling of space to rooms. A carefully placed mirror is as good as another window for improving the light. And because it is not always obvious that we are looking at a reflection in a mirror, and not at a real object, illusionists and magicians employ mirrors for some of their on-stage trickery.

Periscopes also use plane mirrors, angled at 45°. Periscopes are used to look over obstructions, especially if you are not tall enough to see over the heads of people in front of you at a parade or sporting event. Enlarging periscopes that are used in submarines usually contain prisms instead of mirrors.

Curved mirrors

So far we have looked at properties of plane (flat) mirrors. Curved mirrors behave in quite a different way. There are two main types, called concave if they are

---

LAWS OF REFLECTION

At a plane mirror the angles of incidence and reflection are equal. The incident ray, normal, and reflected ray are in the same plane.

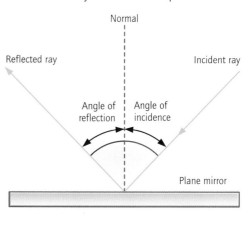

TRY THIS

Multiple reflections

A single mirror produces a single reflection— an image—of an object placed in front of it. Two mirrors provide two images and effectively let you see around corners. In this project, you will investigate multiple reflections from more than one mirror.

What to do

Put two mirrors together with their reflecting surfaces facing each other. Join them down one side with tape (masking tape or Scotch tape will do fine). Stand them up on the sheet of paper as shown in the illustration. Place a coin between the mirrors. How many reflections can you see?

Look carefully in each mirror in turn at the design of the coin. Do they look exactly the same?

Change the coin for a small toy such as a car or a doll. Notice how you can see the front of the object in one mirror and, at the same time, the side of the object in the other mirror. You are, in effect, seeing around a corner. Change the angle between the mirrors by "folding" them closer together and "unfolding" them farther apart. What happens to the images? Try drawing a straight line across the paper, put the folded mirrors across it, and watch how its reflections change as you slightly open and close the mirrors. If you have three mirrors, tape them into a triangle, and put a coin in the middle. How many reflections can you see?

The reflections become more complex if you use a set of three mirrors.

curved inward like the inside of the bowl of a spoon, and convex if they are curved outward like the outside of the bowl of the spoon. The curvature gives such mirrors two further properties. Each has an axis, which is a line at right angles to the mirror that passes through its center. And the radius of curvature is the distance to the mirror from the center of a sphere of which it would form a part. The center of this sphere is also the mirror's center of curvature.

With a concave mirror, rays of light parallel to the axis are reflected to a point known as the focus. For this reason a concave mirror is also called a converging mirror. When a convex mirror reflects parallel rays, however, the reflected rays fan out to form a diverging beam. These rays all appear to come from a single point behind the mirror, which is its focus. A convex mirror is therefore also known as a diverging mirror. The concave mirror has a real focus, while the convex mirror has a virtual focus. In both types of mirror, the focal length—the distance from the mirror to the focus—is half the mirror's radius of curvature.

Images in curved mirrors

The formation of images by curved mirrors is more complicated than with plane mirrors. What happens depends on whether the mirror is concave or convex, and on how far the object is from the mirror. For a concave mirror, there are four different possibilities.

When the object is farther from the mirror than the center of curvature, the image is upside down, smaller than the object, and located in front of the mirror. You can see this for yourself by looking into the bowl of a polished tablespoon from just a few inches away.

When the object is moved closer to the concave mirror's center of curvature, it grows in size until, at exactly the center of curvature, the image (still inverted) is the same size as the object. When the object is even closer to the mirror, between the center of curvature and the focus, the

SNELL'S LAW

Snell's law, the chief law of refraction, states that the sine of the angle of incidence divided by the sine of the angle of refraction is a constant, known as the refractive index.

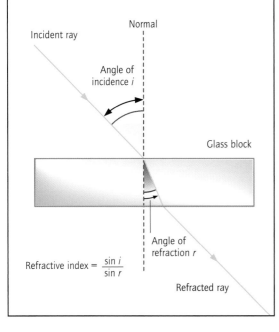

Normal

Incident ray

Angle of incidence i

Glass block

Refractive index $= \dfrac{\sin i}{\sin r}$

Angle of refraction r

Refracted ray

image is still real and inverted but it is now larger than the object. The mirror now magnifies.

Finally, when the object is between the focus and the mirror, the image becomes virtual (is formed behind the mirror), magnified, and the right way up. Such magnified images can be seen in mirrors designed to be used when shaving or putting on makeup.

A convex mirror always produces a reduced, upright virtual image. It is the type used as a driving mirror for motor vehicles. Because the whole scene is reduced in size, it provides a wide angle of view. Both types of curved mirror are used in telescopes (see page 28).

Refraction of light

You may have noticed that a swimming pool looks as if it is not as deep as it really is. And fish in a lake or river appear to be nearer the surface than they really are. The reason for the illusion is that light rays traveling

from underwater objects do not keep going in the same direction when they emerge through the surface and into the air.

A similar effect occurs when light rays pass from air into water. The angle between the incoming ray and the normal (a line at right angles to the surface) is called the angle of incidence. Below the water surface, the angle between the light ray and the normal is called the angle of refraction. When light enters a denser medium, as when it travels from air into water or into glass, the angle of refraction is less than the angle of incidence—the ray is refracted toward the normal. When light travels from one medium into a less dense medium, as from glass into air, the angle of refraction is greater than the angle of incidence—the ray is refracted away from the normal.

As with the reflection of light, there are laws of refraction. The laws concern the angles—not the angles themselves, but a mathematical function called the sine (usually written as sin) of the angle. The chief law says that the sine of the angle of incidence (sin i) divided by the sine of the angle of refraction (sin r) has a constant value for any pair of media. This ratio is known as the refractive index. For air to glass it is

SCIENCE WORDS

- **Concave mirror:** Also called a converging mirror, a type of mirror that causes parallel rays of light to be reflected to a focus in front of the mirror. Its surface curves inward.
- **Convex mirror:** Also called a diverging mirror, a type of mirror that causes parallel rays of light to spread out (diverge) after reflection so that they appear to come from a point (the focus) behind the mirror. Its surface curves outward.
- **Refraction:** The bending of light rays as they pass from one transparent material into another.

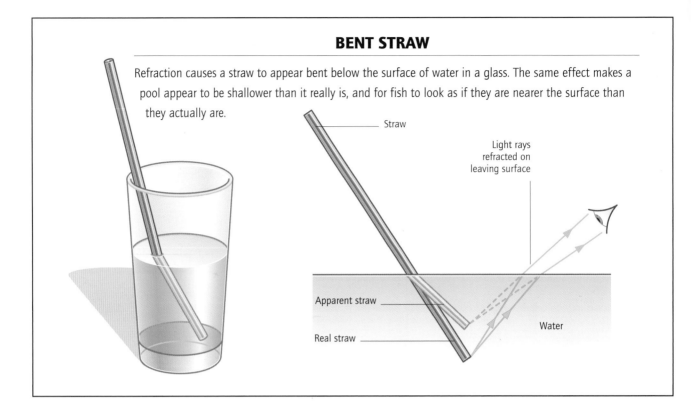

BENT STRAW

Refraction causes a straw to appear bent below the surface of water in a glass. The same effect makes a pool appear to be shallower than it really is, and for fish to look as if they are nearer the surface than they actually are.

Straw

Light rays refracted on leaving surface

Apparent straw

Real straw

Water

about 1.5, and for air to water it is about 1.33. The law is also known as Snell's law, after the Dutch physicist who first formulated it nearly 400 years ago.

Willebrord Snell

Willebrord van Roijen Snell was born in 1580 at Leiden in the Netherlands. He trained in mathematics and physics; and when his father died in 1613, he succeeded him as Professor of Mathematics at the new Leiden University. Snell specialized in land measurement and mapping, and carried out many experiments on light and optics. He discovered his law of refraction in 1621 and introduced the idea of refractive index (now defined as the ratio of the sines of the angles of incidence and refraction). When Snell died in 1626, the results of his work had still not been published. It was later found that the refractive index is also equal to the ratio of the speed of light in the two media concerned.

The second law of refraction states that the incident ray, the normal, and the refracted ray all lie in the same plane (just as with reflection—see page 13).

Bent straws and sunbeams

Refraction can produce some strange effects. If you look at a drinking straw placed in a glass of water, the straw appears to bend below the surface. That is because light rays traveling from the straw and leaving the surface are refracted away from the normal. When we look back along the emerging rays, we see the end of the straw at a position that is apparently nearer the surface (as shown in the illustration at the top of the page).

A similar effect can occur with the setting Sun, when the air near the surface is denser than that above it. Light rays from the Sun are refracted as they pass through this denser air. Again, looking back along the refracted rays, we see the Sun in a different position. As a result, we appear to be able to see the Sun even when it has dropped below the horizon.

In the opposite situation, when light is traveling from dense air through less dense air, refraction also occurs, and a mirage can be the result. In this case the warm air near the ground is less dense than the colder air above it, a condition that often arises in deserts and above the surface of a highway in warm weather. Light rays from a distant object follow a curved path through the warm air. When we look back along these rays, we see an image of the distant object, but the image is upside down and appears to be below the ground surface.

Critical angle

When the angle of incidence reaches a certain value, which physicists call the critical angle, the angle of refraction equals 90°. In other words, the refracted light ray travels along the boundary between the two media. This is called total internal reflection. If the angle of incidence is greater then the critical angle, there is no refraction. The incident ray is then reflected from the surface of the second medium, just as if it had struck a mirror.

Uses of refraction

The major practical use of refraction is in lenses and in the many different types of instruments and devices that employ them. These include cameras, telescopes, microscopes, binoculars and projectors (see pages 26 to 31). Optical prisms also make use of refraction (see pages 18 to 19).

A more recent application is fiber optics, in which light is "piped" along a bundle of thin fibers of glass or plastic. A succession of refractions and internal reflections occur along the length of each fiber so that most of the light entering at one end comes out at the other end. Fiber optics are used in medical endoscopes for making examinations inside a patient's body and for long-distance telephone cables in which signals are transmitted as a series of coded flashes of light. Several thousand telephone conversations can be sent at the same time along a single optic fiber.

TRY THIS

Hidden money

When light rays pass from one transparent medium into another, they are bent. This process is called refraction. In this project, you will use refraction to make a coin appear.

What to do

Put a large, shallow bowl on a table, and place a coin on the bottom of the bowl between the center and the edge nearest to you. Now back off slowly, while looking at the coin, until the coin goes out of sight behind the edge of the bowl. Ask your friend to slowly fill the bowl with water. The vanished coin comes back into view.

The water refracts light rays from the coin. As the rays leave the surface of the water, they are bent toward you. For the same reason, fish in a pond always look nearer and not as far below the surface as they really are. Herons and other birds that catch fish have to take this into account and "aim off" when they try to grab their prey.

Stand where you cannot see the coin in the empty bowl.

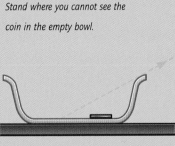

When the bowl is filled with water, refraction lets you see the coin.

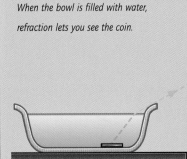

PRISMS AND LENSES

Prisms are the best-known light benders. Refraction bends a light ray when it enters a prism and then bends it again when it leaves. More importantly, it bends different colors of light to a different extent. In fact, a triangular prism can split white light from the Sun into all the colors of the rainbow—a range of hues called the solar spectrum.

One of the most important experiments in physics took place in a darkened room in Cambridge, England, in about 1665. The physicist Isaac Newton (1643–1727) allowed a beam of sunlight through a hole in the drapes and shone it onto a glass prism. To his surprise, parallel bands of rainbow colors appeared on the opposite wall. From this observation Newton concluded that sunlight consists of a mixture of colors that the

prism had separated. When he selected just one of the colors and passed it through a second prism, there was no further change.

A triangular glass prism splits a beam of white light into a spectrum of colors that ranges from red, through orange, yellow, green, blue, and indigo, to violet. These are the colors of the rainbow.

SINGLE-LENS REFLEX

There are two types of reflector in a modern single-lens reflex (SLR) camera: a mirror and a five-sided prism called a pentaprism. Light entering the camera through the lens is first reflected upward by the mirror. Then two more reflections inside the pentaprism direct the light out of the viewfinder and into the photographer's eye. A pentaprism is used (and not another mirror) because the image leaving the lens is upside down, and the double reflection in the pentaprism turns the image right side up again.

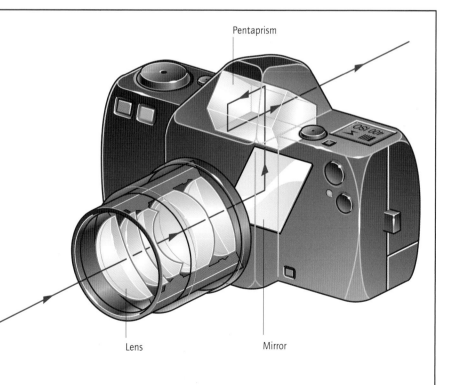

Pentaprism

Lens

Mirror

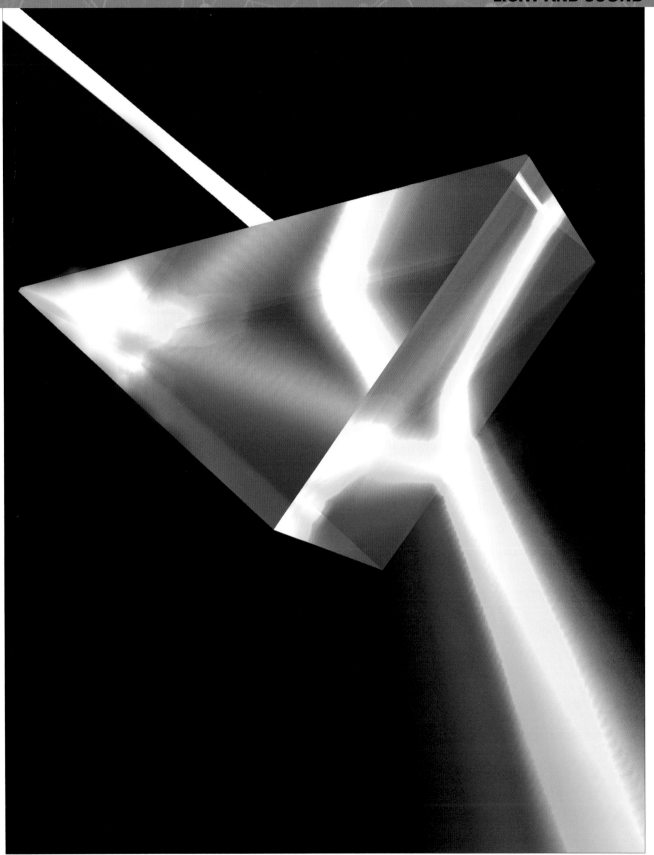

Modern physics can easily explain what happened in Newton's room. White light is made up of a mixture of the colors of the rainbow, ranging from red to violet with all the other colors in between. As each color enters the prism, it is refracted (bent). But red light is not bent as much as violet light. As a result, the red and violet emerge from the prism at different angles (and the in-between colors emerge at in-between angles). This has the effect of spreading white light's component colors into a spectrum. The colors are red, orange, yellow, green, blue, indigo, and violet.

This special sort of refraction by a prism is known as dispersion. And the different colors produced are called a spectrum. This accounts for the colors that can sometimes been seen when sunlight shines through a crystal glass or ornamental light fitting. It also accounts for the formation of rainbows (see page 22).

A water droplet viewed through a magnifying glass. The type of lens used in magnifying glasses is a convex or converging lens.

Uses of prisms

Prisms are used in several scientific instruments, such as spectrographs, as well as in periscopes and binoculars. But perhaps the most common use today is in the single-lens reflex (SLR) camera. Everyday prisms, such as the one Newton used, are triangular in shape. But this camera uses a prism with five faces, called a pentaprism.

Lenses

There are two main kinds of lens, named either after their shape or after the effect they have on rays of light that pass through them. A lens whose surfaces bulge outward is called a convex lens (like a convex mirror). This is the type of lens that is used as a magnifying glass. But because parallel light rays that

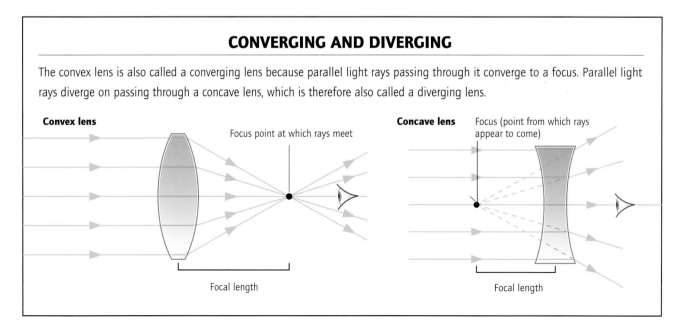

CONVERGING AND DIVERGING

The convex lens is also called a converging lens because parallel light rays passing through it converge to a focus. Parallel light rays diverge on passing through a concave lens, which is therefore also called a diverging lens.

Convex lens

Focus point at which rays meet

Focal length

Concave lens

Focus (point from which rays appear to come)

Focal length

pass through a convex lens converge (come together) to a focus on the other side of the lens, a convex lens is also commonly referred to as a converging lens.

A lens whose surfaces are curved inward is called a concave lens (like a concave mirror). It is the type of lens used in eyeglasses for shortsighted people. Parallel light rays passing through a concave lens diverge (spread out), and the focus is on the same side as the incident light. For this reason, a concave lens is also referred to as a diverging lens.

Larger and smaller

We have already noted that a convex lens can be used as a magnifying glass. But how exactly does this work?. Parallel light rays from an object converge toward a focus, and when we look back along these rays, we see a magnified image of the object. With a concave lens the light rays diverge toward the observer's eye. Looking back along these rays reveals a diminished image of the object. Artists and designers sometimes use a diverging lens, which they call a reducing glass, to check how a large image will appear when it is reduced in size.

Faulty lenses

If you look at an object through a simple convex lens, you can often see colored fringes around the edge of the image. This effect is called chromatic aberration

TRY THIS

Reversing arrow
This very simple project can be put in the form of a puzzle: how can you reverse the direction of an arrow without touching it?

What to do
Use a colored pen to draw a fat horizontal arrow on a piece of cardboard, pointing to the left. Prop the cardboard upright against a drinking glass. How can you reverse the arrow without touching the paper?

Fill another glass with water, and stand it several inches in front of the cardboard. Look at the arrow. It is now pointing to the right! What happens is that the glass of water acts like a fat lens and produces a reversed image of the arrow. Place the glass of water nearer the paper, and the arrow will go back to pointing to the left.

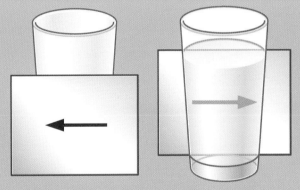

Stand a glass of water in front of the arrow to reverse its direction.

SCIENCE WORDS

- **Concave lens:** Also called a diverging lens, a type of lens that causes parallel rays of light to spread out (diverge) as if coming from a point (the focus) behind the lens. Its surfaces curve inward.
- **Convex lens:** Also called a converging lens, a type of lens that causes parallel rays of light to converge to a point (the focus) in front of the lens. Its surfaces curve outward.

(any fault in a lens is known as an aberration). It happens because the edges of the lens refract blue light more than red light so that the two colors are focused at different points. It can be corrected by adding a concave lens made from a different kind of glass, which makes the blue rays diverge and come to the same focus as the red rays. The resulting combination is called an achromatic lens (or achromat).

LIGHT AND COLOR

White light is actually made up of a mixture of all the colors of the rainbow, as we saw on the previous pages. So why do colored objects look colored when they are illuminated with white light? And why do most colored objects change color when they are illuminated with colored light?

A bright rainbow arches down. Around this bow, at a slightly greater height, a faint secondary rainbow can just be seen. Its colors are in the opposite order from those in the primary rainbow.

COLORED OBJECTS

White light is a mixture of all colors. When it shines on something colored, the object absorbs all colors except its own. This color is reflected to the eyes of the observer. A little of the neighboring colors in the spectrum are reflected as well, particularly from yellow objects.

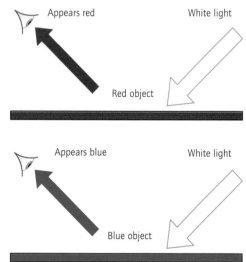

Appears red — White light — Red object

Appears blue — White light — Blue object

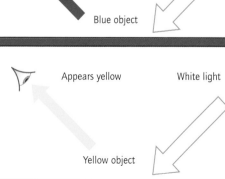

Appears yellow — White light — Yellow object

The illustration on the left explains why colored objects look colored. When white light illuminates a red object, for example, most of the light is absorbed by the surface of the object. Most—but not all. The red component of the white light is reflected, along with a little orange. As a result, the object appears to our eyes to be red. Similarly, a blue object reflects mostly blue light, and a yellow object reflects mostly yellow.

This explanation works only for white light. Illuminating objects with colored light can have strange effects. Try looking at the colors of cars and trucks under yellow sodium streetlights, and you will not be able to get the colors right. In fact, only yellow vehicles still look yellow.

Mixing colored lights

We have seen that white light is a mixture of the seven colors of the rainbow. So it should come as no surprise to learn that mixing all seven colors in the right amounts produces white light. But not all seven colors are needed. You can make white light by mixing only three colors, which are known as the primary colors of light.

Light's primary colors are red, blue, and green. All three mixed together make white. But the primary colors can be mixed in pairs to make three more colors, called secondary colors. Red and green light mix to make yellow, green and blue mix to make a brighter blue called cyan, and blue and red mix to make a pinkish red called magenta.

A mixture of the three secondary colors again produces white light. In fact, careful mixing of the three primary or secondary colors of light will produce any color you can think of. If you look at a television picture up real close, you will see that it is made up of lots of tiny colored dots. Look even closer, and you will see that there are only three kinds of colored dot: red, green, and blue—the primary colors. In this way, the correct mixture of dots produces the complete range of colors on the TV screen. The colors of a color transparency photograph are produced in much the same way. Because the colors are added to make new colors, this type of color mixing is called the additive process.

Mixing colored paints

So far we have looked at the mixing of colored lights. More familiar to most people is the effect of mixing paints, inks, and other pigments. If you mix all the colors in a paintbox, you will get a muddy black color.

As with colored lights, colored paints have three primary colors: yellow, cyan, and magenta (exactly the same as the secondary colors of light). A mixture of all three primary colors produces black. Mixing the primary colors in pairs produces the secondary colors of paint: yellow and magenta mix to make red, magenta and cyan mix to make blue, and cyan and yellow mix to produce green. Notice that the secondary colors of paint are the same as the primary colors of light.

When yellow and magenta paints are mixed, this has the effect of removing blue and green from black, which leaves red. Similarly, mixing magenta and cyan removes red and green to leave blue, and mixing cyan and yellow removes red and blue to leave green. Artists learn how to make other colors by mixing. In fact, some artists make most of the colors they need by combining them. Because mixing colored paints effectively removes colors from black, it is called the subtractive process.

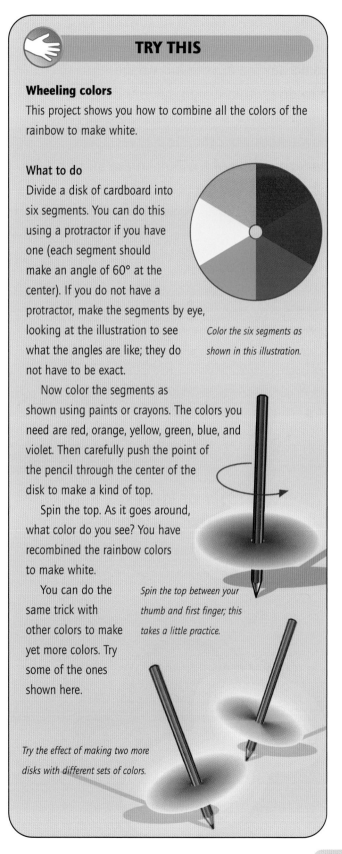

TRY THIS

Wheeling colors
This project shows you how to combine all the colors of the rainbow to make white.

What to do
Divide a disk of cardboard into six segments. You can do this using a protractor if you have one (each segment should make an angle of 60° at the center). If you do not have a protractor, make the segments by eye, looking at the illustration to see what the angles are like; they do not have to be exact.

Color the six segments as shown in this illustration.

Now color the segments as shown using paints or crayons. The colors you need are red, orange, yellow, green, blue, and violet. Then carefully push the point of the pencil through the center of the disk to make a kind of top.

Spin the top. As it goes around, what color do you see? You have recombined the rainbow colors to make white.

You can do the same trick with other colors to make yet more colors. Try some of the ones shown here.

Spin the top between your thumb and first finger; this takes a little practice.

Try the effect of making two more disks with different sets of colors.

THE HUMAN EYE

Light has been defined as the only type of radiation that we can see. But we could not see anything if we did not have eyes. The human eye is a natural application of a lens. Understanding how lenses work therefore gives us an understanding of the human eye and of some of the defects of human vision and how to correct them.

The main parts of the human eye are shown in the illustration below. The lens and its supporting structures divide the eyeball into two unequal chambers. The front chamber contains a watery liquid called aqueous humor. The jellylike vitreous humor fills the larger chamber. The eyeball itself is transparent at the front, at the cornea, so that light can enter. A thin layer of tears keeps the cornea moist.

The lens is supported by ciliary muscles, which can also pull on the lens to change its shape to focus on

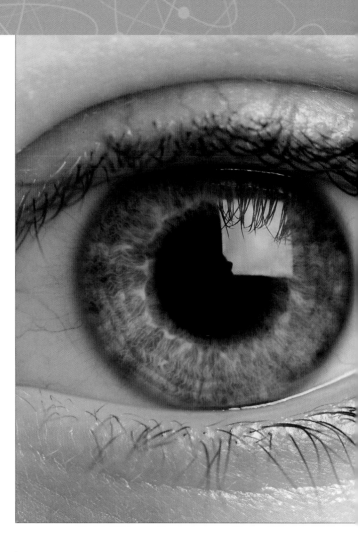

The colored part of the eye is the iris, which surrounds the black pupil. Light from everything we see passes through the pupil and into the eyeball.

ANATOMY OF THE EYE

Important parts of the eye include the lens and the cornea. Both help in focusing, although only the lens is adjustable—it does most of the work.

Ciliary muscle

Iris

Cornea

Pupil

Aqueous humor

Lens

Vitreous humor

Retina

Optic nerve

---

objects. The lens is stretched and made thinner when we look at distant objects, and allowed to get thicker (by relaxing the ciliary muscles) when we look at nearby objects. The colored iris in front of the lens has a central hole called the pupil. The iris can change size to vary the size of the pupil. The pupil is large in dim light, so that it can admit as much light as possible, but in bright light the iris closes down to make the pupil much smaller.

Light detection

The light-sensitive retina lines the inside of the eyeball, and the lens focuses an upside-down image of objects

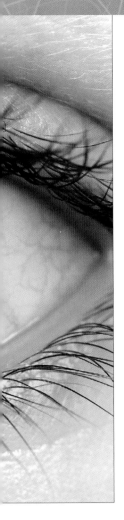

onto the retina. There the light triggers nerve impulses, which pass along the optic nerve to the brain. The brain then combines the impulses from both eyes, converts them into "pictures" that we can see, and turns them the right way up.

Eye defects

The two upper diagrams on the right show a normal eye and how it forms images. In two of the commonest defects of eyesight, light rays are not focused correctly on the retina. In a longsighted person, the eyeball is too short front-to-back. As a result, the eye's lens tries to focus light rays at a point behind the retina. This condition is corrected with eyeglasses made from convex lenses or by convex contact lenses. They make the rays converge in focus onto the retina.

In a shortsighted person, the eyeball is too long front-to-back. The eye's lens brings light rays to a focus that lies in front of the retina. To improve their vision, shortsighted people wear eyeglasses made from concave lenses or concave contact lenses. They make the rays diverge slightly, so that they come to the right focus on the retina.

Another common eye defect, called astigmatism, arises when the transparent cornea at the front of the eyeball is not perfectly spherical. When looking at a cross like a plus sign (+) with an astigmatic eye, either the upright part of the cross is in focus and the horizontal part is not, or vice versa. The condition is corrected with eyeglasses or contact lenses that have a similar fault, but at right angles to that of the eye. Such lenses are called anastigmatic.

VISION IN FOCUS

In a normal human eye, the lens produces an image that is much smaller than actual size. In a longsighted eye, light rays are focused behind the retina. This can be corrected with convex lenses. In a shortsighted eye, the rays are focused in front of the retina; concave lenses correct this condition.

Normal eye

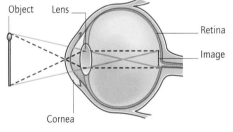

Image formation

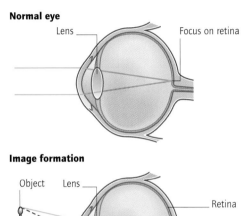

Longsighted eye

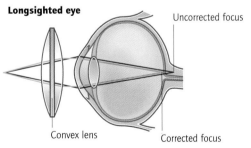

Shortsighted eye

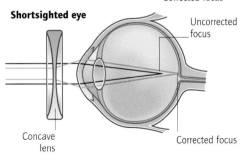

The main components of optical devices are mirrors, lenses, and prisms. The workings of all of them have been dealt with earlier in this book. Now we look at how they are put to practical use in various kinds of optical instrument.

Nowadays nearly everyone owns at least one camera, which is therefore the most common optical device. In many ways a camera works like the human eye (described on the previous pages). It has a lens, a variable aperture, and a light-sensitive surface. The lens focuses the image, the aperture controls the amount of light entering the camera, and the film records the image focused onto it by the lens. The image is actually

SIMPLE CAMERA

A camera is basically a lightproof box that holds light-sensitive film. A lens focuses an image of the object to be photographed onto the film. The lens can be screwed in or out slightly to focus the image. An adjustable aperture, called an iris diaphragm, can be altered in size to control the amount of light entering the camera. The amount of light that falls on the film is also determined by the length of time for which the shutter is open.

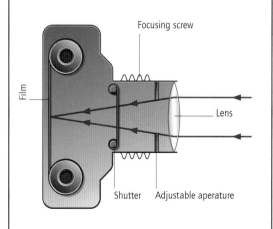

Focusing screw

Film

Lens

Shutter   Adjustable aperature

upside down, but of course this does not matter. In addition, a camera has a shutter that controls the amount of time (in fractions of a second) for which light is allowed into the camera and onto the film.

In order to focus the object being photographed—depending on how far away it is—the lens can be moved farther from or nearer to the film. This is usually achieved by rotating the lens mount, which has a fine screw thread. In very old cameras, as well as some specialized modern ones, the lens is mounted on a bellows arrangement and racks backward or forward to focus the camera. In this respect, the camera is different from the human eye, in which the lens changes shape in order to focus. But there are animals that focus their eyes just like a camera by moving the

TRY THIS

Camera in a can

Lenses work by bending light rays. One of their best-known uses is in a camera. In this project, you will make a camera with no lens at all!

What to do

Wash out an empty tin can thoroughly, and dry it, being careful in case there is a sharp edge. Using the hammer and nail, punch a very small hole in the center of the closed end of the can. You may want to get an adult to help you do this. Cut a square of tissue paper larger than the diameter of the can, and use a rubber band to put it over the open end. Cut a piece of construction paper big enough to go all around the can and about 2 in (5 cm) longer than the can. Wrap it around the can, and secure it with tape. Keep the paper flush with the closed end, and let it project beyond the tissue paper, forming a kind of hood.

Make a small hole in the base of the can, and stretch tissue paper over the open end.

With the hole away from you, point your can camera at an object that is well lit. It will work best out of doors. An image of the object will appear upside-down on the tissue paper "screen." The tiny hole acts as if it were a lens, focusing rays of light from the object onto the screen. But just as in a real camera, the image is upside-down. The images formed in the backs of our eyes are also upside-down, but fortunately our brain turns them right side up.

Turn the paper-covered end toward you, and wrap black paper around the can.

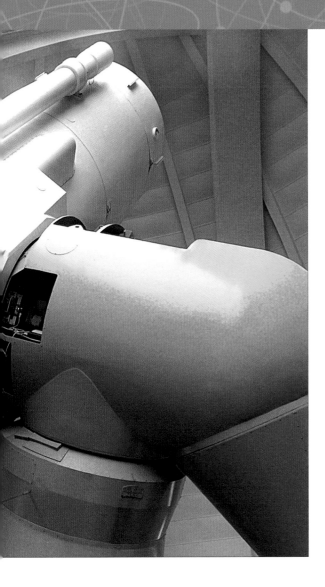

A 2-meter reflecting telescope at an observatory. The figure refers to the diameter of the primary mirror in the instrument.

lens in and out—an octopus, for example, can do this.

A device called a viewfinder allows the photographer to aim the camera accurately. The viewfinder of a simple camera is a pair of small lenses. In a single-lens reflex camera a pentaprism forms the viewfinder (see page 18). Some cameras have interchangeable lenses— alternative lenses for different tasks. They range from wide-angle lenses with short focal lengths to long-focus telephoto lenses for taking closeups of distant objects.

Digital cameras have dispensed with film altogether and use computer technology to record images, but they still rely on traditional lens systems to form the image.

REFLECTING TELESCOPES

Professional astronomers use reflecting telescopes to study the heavens. Light from distant objects first strikes a curved primary mirror, which brings the light to a focus, where it is viewed by an eyepiece. In most designs, the light is diverted to the focus by a smaller, secondary mirror. The Schmidt camera is used mainly for photographing large areas of the night sky. Its primary mirror is an easy-to-make spherical mirror; and to avoid spherical aberration, light first passes through a specially shaped corrector plate. Photographic film is placed at the focus to record the image. The Newtonian reflector avoids spherical aberration by having a primary mirror with a cross-section in the form of a parabola—more steeply curved near the center than at the edges. Light focused by the primary mirror is directed to a focus at the side of the tube by a flat mirror placed at 45°. The Maksutov telescope uses a corrector plate to overcome spherical aberration. The secondary mirror is a silvered spot on the back of the corrector plate, which reflects light back down the tube through a hole in the center of the primary mirror.

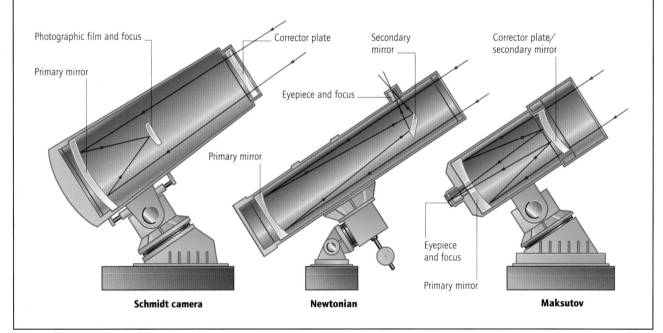

Schmidt camera   **Newtonian**   **Maksutov**

Objects at a distance

A telephoto lens for use with a camera is basically a type of telescope. The more usual kind of telescope consists of a long tube with a lens at each end. The front lens is the objective lens, and the rear one is the eyepiece. With two convex lenses the image is upside down, although this does not usually matter in astronomy A third convex lens may be positioned inside the telescope tube, which will turn the image the correct way up.

If the eyepiece is a concave lens, the image is the right way up. This type is known as a Galilean telescope, after the Italian scientist Galileo Galilei (1564-1642), who used this same design in his pioneering astronomical studies nearly 400 years ago. A pair of Galilean telescopes mounted side by side form opera glasses, sometimes used by people seated toward the back of a theater to get a better view of the performance.

Paired telescopes are also employed in binoculars. Powerful telescopes are long and difficult to hold without a stand or a mounting. And, as we have seen, they produce an inverted image. All of these difficulties are overcome in prismatic binoculars, in which each telescope has a pair of prisms that "fold" the optical path back and forth to shorten it. They are also arranged at right angles to each other, so that the final image is the right way up.

Telescopes for astronomy

Modern astronomers need really powerful telescopes. These types have curved mirrors instead of lenses. Large mirrors are easier to make and are much lighter in weight than are big lenses (see the picture on pages 12–13). There are various designs of mirror telescope, which are called reflecting telescopes or reflectors (see left); telescopes with lenses are known as refracting telescopes or refractors. Isaac Newton (1643–1727) made the first reflector. It had a single curved mirror at the bottom of a tube, with a small plane mirror angled near the other end. Light rays are reflected by the plane mirror to the eyepiece at the side of the telescope.

The latest types of astronomical telescope used by professional astronomers have mirrors of up to 33 feet (10 meters) across. Computer-controlled arms below the mirror adjust its shape to keep its curvature exactly right. Some very large mirrors are composed of many hexagonal panels, resembling a honeycomb. A computer controls the positions of the panels. Astronomical telescopes are mounted in large domed buildings, which can be rotated to aim the telescope at any part of the sky. The observatories are often located on high peaks, where the air is clearer, resulting in better images.

Very small objects

Microscopes produce enlarged images of very small objects. The very first microscopes had a single, small convex lens. This type, called the simple microscope, was first made by a Dutch cloth-seller named Anton van Leeuwenhoek (1632–1723) in about 1670. His best instruments magnified more than 260 times, and with

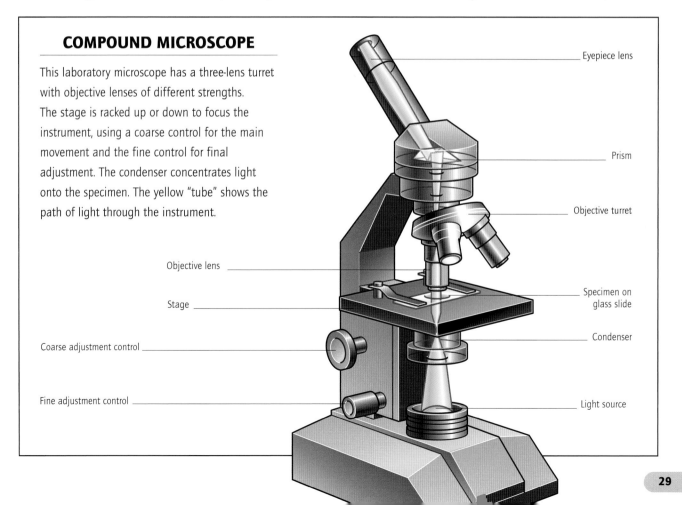

COMPOUND MICROSCOPE

This laboratory microscope has a three-lens turret with objective lenses of different strengths. The stage is racked up or down to focus the instrument, using a coarse control for the main movement and the fine control for final adjustment. The condenser concentrates light onto the specimen. The yellow "tube" shows the path of light through the instrument.

Eyepiece lens

Prism

Objective turret

Specimen on glass slide

Condenser

Light source

Objective lens

Stage

Coarse adjustment control

Fine adjustment control

them he was able to examine bacteria and blood cells.

To obtain higher magnifications, a compound microscope is used. It has a small but powerful objective lens. The image formed by the objective (a convex lens) is further enlarged by the eyepiece lens, also convex. In use, the microscope is adjusted so that the object being examined is just beyond the focal length of the objective lens. This produces an enlarged inverted image inside the microscope tube. The image is just inside the focal length of the eyepiece lens, which acts like a magnifying glass to produce a greatly enlarged final image. The image remains inverted, but this seldom matters in most applications.

Most laboratory microscopes have a turret with two or three objectives of different magnifying powers. The operator rotates the turret to bring the required lens into position. A glass slide on which is placed the specimen to be examined is mounted on a stage and illuminated from below by a bulb or by light reflected from a curved mirror. A pair of lenses called a condenser concentrates the light on the specimen. For some studies, such as the examination of geological

rock specimens, a binocular microscope is often used. This is essentially a compound microscope equipped with two eyepieces.

Projecting images

We saw earlier how a camera works. One type of photograph that can be produced is a color transparency, commonly known as a slide. A slide can be viewed by holding it up to the light, but of course the image is very small and difficult to examine in detail. A better way of viewing it is to project an enlarged image of the slide onto a screen. This is the function of a slide projector.

In a slide projector, condenser lenses concentrate light from an electric lamp onto the slide and illuminate it evenly. Some condensers also incorporate a heat filter to avoid damaging the slide. The light passes through the slide, and the projector lens forms the image on the screen. The lens can be moved in or out slightly in order to focus the image. The image is actually upside down, which is why slides have to be inserted upside down into the projector.

SLIDE PROJECTOR

The optical system of a slide projector includes a curved mirror that acts as a reflector to direct light from a lamp onto the condenser. The condenser evens out the light, which then passes through the slide. Finally, a lens projects an enlarged image of the slide onto a distant screen.

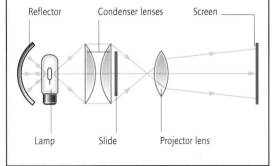

LASER LIGHT

Atoms in the ruby crystal emit light when they absorb energy from the flash tube. This light then stimulates more atoms to give off light, which bounces between the mirrors at the ends of the crystal. Coherent red laser light leaves through a hole in one mirror.

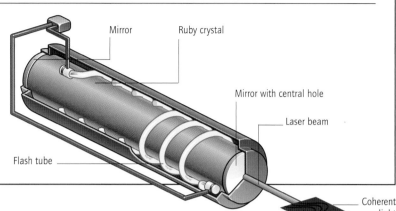

Mirror Ruby crystal

Mirror with central hole

Laser beam

Flash tube

Coherent light

A movie projector is optically much the same. It has in addition a mechanism to move the film through the projector and a shutter that opens and closes rapidly (usually 24 times every second). Each individual picture, or frame, of the film is stationary when the shutter is open. Then, when the shutter closes, the film moves on to the next frame. So when we go to the movies, we are actually seeing 24 still pictures each second. But our brain ignores the brief black screens between consecutive images, and we "see" continuous

movement. A movie camera has a similar shutter arrangement, but in every other respect it is optically like the still camera described earlier.

Lasers

Another quite different use of light is the laser, a device that produces an intense beam of light that is all of the same wavelength, and whose waves are perfectly in step (coherent).

"Laser" is an abbreviation of the jawbreaking term "light amplification by stimulated emission of radiation". The laser material can be a solid, such as a ruby crystal, or a gas, such as a mixture of helium and neon. Light energy from a flash tube energizes atoms of the laser material. Some of these atoms give off light, which stimulates more atoms to emit light in the same direction. Mirrors at each end of the laser bounce the light backward and forward, so that it gets stronger and stronger. The laser beam emerges from a central hole in one of the mirrors. Lasers have found many different applications in medicine, industry, and communications. They are also used to scan compact disks in CD players and in computers.

An industrial laser cutting through a sheet of steel. Lasers offer the advantage of greater precision over mechanical cutting methods, and are also used for welding.

SOUND WAVES

The air that surrounds us gives us more than life—it also gives us the rich world of sounds. Our nerves and brains convert those sounds into the experience of music, voices, and the activity of the world around us.

Sound is a disturbance of the air. We are able to hear things because there is air between us and the things that cause the sound.

Sound is a particular kind of disturbance: it is a vibration. Not all disturbances of the air, however, are vibrations. The wind consists of a movement of the air from one place to another, revealed by the movement of clouds across the sky or by scraps of paper blown along a street. But the movement of air that carries a sound is not so obvious because it does not make the air move as a whole. Instead, the tiny particles, known as molecules, that the air is composed of, vibrate individually—at each place they move backward and then forward without any overall change in their position (unless there is a wind blowing).

What happens in a wave

Although we cannot see air, we can get an impression of what the vibrations of molecules in air are like by comparing them with the movement of water. Water moves from place to place in rivers and streams, in ocean currents, and in the flow from a faucet. These water movements are like the movement of air in winds. But waves in water are different. There can be waves even in calm water—on a lake, for example. These waves move along, but the water does not move along as a whole. A boat floating on the lake is not carried along; instead, it bobs up and down. As a wave passes beneath the boat, the individual molecules of water make a circular movement, going backward and forward and up and down. When the wave has passed, the molecules will have scarcely changed their positions and neither will the boat. Sounds are waves in the air.

A sound wave in still air travels on, while individual air molecules merely vibrate around a particular position.

Push–pull waves

In a sound wave, the molecules of air get more or less crowded together. You can see a similar sort of wave in a long, flexible spring, such as the toy springs that "walk" downstairs by themselves. Imagine the spring is hanging from one end. Jiggling the bottom end of the spring squeezes the coils of the wire closer together, with each coil pushing the next above it, and waves of compression move up the spring, separated by zones where the coils are momentarily stretched.

Air acts as if it were a spring. When something vibrating, such as the skin of a drum, briefly "jiggles" it, waves of compression travel outward. In these zones of compression, molecules in the air are crowded together. Between adjacent zones of compression the molecules are more thinly spread—the air is "rarefied." As the waves pass by, the molecules do not change

32

This explosion is an uncontrolled release of energy that creates a devastating blast wave in the air. The blast consists of air rushing outward and travels only a short way. But beyond the blast sound waves are created that consist of air vibrating backward and forward. These waves travel long distances.

their position—they vibrate backward and forward, first in the direction the wave is moving, and then in the opposite direction.

Sound, noise, and hearing

How we perceive a sound depends on our ears and brains. We cannot hear vibrations of the air that are very slow or very fast. We cannot hear vibrations in which the molecules make only very small movements; and vibrations that are very large hurt our ears and can even damage our sense of hearing, perhaps permanently.

Sounds vary not only in their loudness and pitch, but also in their distinctive quality, or "color," which is called "timbre" (pronounced tam-ber). Notes played on

a piano, a violin, and a flute sound quite different even when they all have the same pitch; the distinctive quality that enables us to recognize the instrument is the timbre. These differences all result from the different and complicated vibrations of the air molecules. Sounds from most instruments have a definite pitch—each note produced is distinct and different. A mixture of sounds with no definite pitch, as in an explosion, is called noise.

COMPRESSION WAVES

When sound radiates outward from a source, air does not move away from the source as a whole. Instead, the particles in the air, called molecules, vibrate backward and forward. Where the molecules are squeezed closer together, they are said to be compressed. Where they move apart, they are described as rarefied. The movement of the sound wave is the movement of this pattern of crowding and spreading out. It is like a "Mexican wave" in a football stadium: spectators do not leave their seats, but stand and sit in succession so that a wave of motion runs through the crowd.

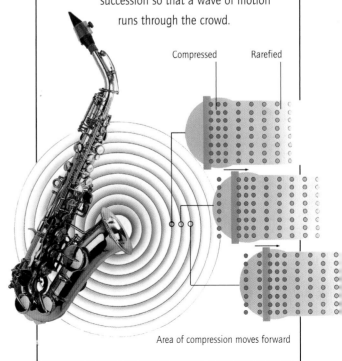

Compressed   Rarefied

Area of compression moves forward

PROPERTIES OF SOUND WAVES

We can best understand the behavior of sound by thinking of it as a wave motion. Sound waves, like other waves, have certain important features, such as their wavelength and frequency, and the speed at which they travel.

To understand the behavior of sound waves, it is necessary to know something about waves in general. Water waves give the clearest illustration. The distance from one peak of a wave to the next (or from one trough to the next) is called the wavelength.

In sound waves, there are places, like the peaks and troughs of water waves, where the air molecules have shifted the most from their initial positions in the forward direction, and others where they have shifted the most in the backward direction. The distance from any one "peak" to the next, or from any one "trough" to the next one, is the wavelength of the sound wave.

The number of waves passing a given point every second is called the frequency of the wave. The

frequency of the wave multiplied by its wavelength is the speed of the wave (speed = number of waves passing per second * the length of each wave). Under the same conditions all sound waves move at approximately the same speed. This means that higher-frequency waves have shorter wavelengths, and lower-frequency waves have longer wavelengths.

Waves in water can be large or small. The height of a wave above the level of calm water is called its amplitude. The amplitude of a sound wave is the distance the air molecules move from their rest positions. The more violent the disturbance that causes the sound, the greater the amplitude and the louder the sound.

The speed of sound

Sound must have something to travel in, and it travels faster in some substances than in others. The speed of sound in air, for example, is about 1,080 feet per second (about 330 meters per second). As a result, it takes approximately 5 seconds for sound to travel 1

SCIENCE WORDS

- **Amplitude:** The intensity of a wave. The amplitude of a sound wave is directly related to its loudness.
- **Decibel (dB):** A unit of loudness equal to one tenth of a bel. If a sound is 10 dB louder than another one, it is 10 times as intense; if it is 20 dB louder, it is 10 * 10 = 100 times as intense, and so on.
- **Frequency:** For a sound wave the number of times per second that the air molecules (or the molecules of whatever material the wave is traveling through) vibrate.
- **Wavelength:** The distance between two successive locations where a wave is at its maximum intensity.

Sound waves can be focused just as light waves can. The curved walls of the Whispering Gallery in London's St. Paul's Cathedral reflect sounds so that someone whispering on one side of the gallery can be heard on the other.

mile (or 3 seconds to travel 1 kilometer).

Sound travels faster in liquids than it does in air and other gases. In pure water, its speed is about 4,900 ft/s (about 1,500 m/s) and slightly higher in seawater. Sound travels fastest of all in solids. Its speed is about 16,500 ft/s (5,000 m/s) in steel, and in a hard rock such as granite it is about 19,700 ft/s (6,000 m/s). The sound of an approaching train, for example, can be heard as vibrations of the railroad lines before the sound of the locomotive reaches our ears through the air. That is because sound travels 15 times faster in steel than it does in air.

Decibels

Scientists measure loudness of sounds in decibels (symbol dB). The decibel equals one-tenth of another unit called the bel, named for Alexander Graham Bell (1847–1922), inventor of the telephone. A difference of 10 dB corresponds to a ratio in loudness of 10 times. That is, the intensity of a sound of 70 dB is 10 times that of a sound of 60 dB. The sound level in a busy city street is typically around 70 dB. In a disco or a rock concert the sound level is around 110 dB. A supersonic fighter taking off 550 yards (500 meters) away puts out an ear-splitting 120 dB.

The loudness of a sound wave is related to its energy. This energy, in turn, depends on the mass of air molecules set in motion by a vibrating object. The larger the mass

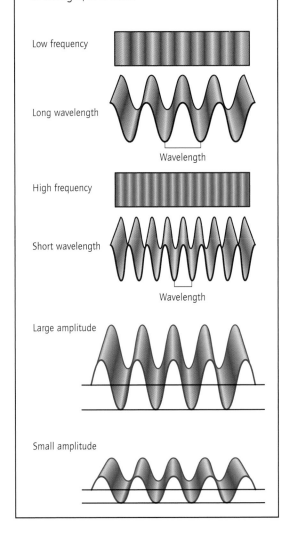

FREQUENCY, WAVELENGTH, AND AMPLITUDE

For any wave, the wavelength is the distance from one peak (or trough) to the next. The shorter the wavelength, the more waves pass a fixed point each second—that is, the higher the frequency. Amplitude is related to the intensity, or strength, of a wave.

Low frequency

Long wavelength

Wavelength

High frequency

Short wavelength

Wavelength

Large amplitude

Small amplitude

of air, the louder the sound. For example, the vibrating diaphragm in the earpiece of a telephone is too small to vibrate a large mass of air, so it cannot produce loud sounds. But the diaphragms in a rock band's large loudspeakers can pump out more than 110 dB.

VIBRATING STRINGS

Stringed instruments date from before the beginning of recorded history. Taut strings can be plucked, struck, or rubbed with bows to create sounds as different as those of the harp and the violin. They can produce this variety of sound because it is possible for many waves to vibrate along the length of a single string at the same time.

Many types of musical instrument have taut strings that vibrate when they are struck or plucked or rubbed. Each stretched string vibrates with a certain frequency that is natural to it. This in turn sets the air in motion, making it vibrate at the same frequency as the string does. The vibration dies away if the string is

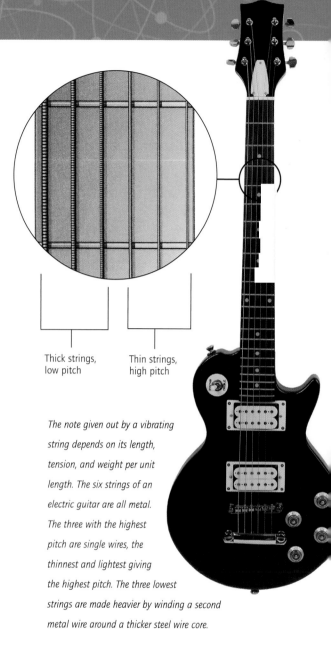

Thick strings, low pitch   Thin strings, high pitch

The note given out by a vibrating string depends on its length, tension, and weight per unit length. The six strings of an electric guitar are all metal. The three with the highest pitch are single wires, the thinnest and lightest giving the highest pitch. The three lowest strings are made heavier by winding a second metal wire around a thicker steel wire core.

VIBRATING STRING

The simplest way in which a string can vibrate is when there are just two stationary points, called nodes, one at each of its ends, and the maximum movement is at the center, called the antinode. The vibration of the string sets up vibrations of the air, or sound waves, with the same frequency.

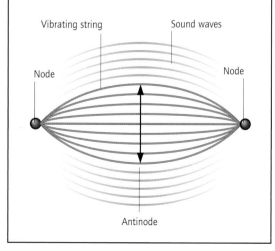

Vibrating string   Sound waves

Node   Node

Antinode

---

plucked or struck once. But if the string is scraped with a bow (which is a set of taut horsehair strings stretched by a flexible wooden rod), the continued force keeps the string vibrating. The string makes a sustained note, but the note is still of the same frequency.

In any note produced in this way there are actually other, higher, frequencies mixed in with the main frequency, which is known as the fundamental. However, to understand how musicians produce different notes on stringed instruments, it is easier if we start by imagining that the fundamental is the only frequency present.

Numbers and harmonies

The frequency of vibration of a string depends on its tension. If you pull the string more tautly, the pitch rises. It falls again as you slacken the string. When a guitarist tunes up, you can hear the notes from the strings rising and falling. Rock guitarists make use of this effect when they use the tremolo arm. It "wobbles" the bridge, the device on the body of the guitar to which the strings are attached. That alters the tension of the strings slightly, making the pitches of the notes being played "wobble" too.

When the tension in a string does not vary, the pitch of the note it gives out depends on its length. The shorter the string is made, the higher the note it produces. A harp has its characteristic shape because it is simply a set of strings, each with its own fixed length and providing a note in the range that is covered by the instrument. Players of bowed instruments vary the length of the strings by pressing the strings against the neck of the instrument, known as "stopping" them, at varying positions. Guitarists do the same, but there are ridges or bars called frets set into the neck of the guitar, providing a fixed endpoint for the string.

One of the earliest discoveries of mathematical patterns in nature was made by the Greek philosopher Pythagoras (*c.* 570–*c.* 500 B.C.) in the 6th century B.C. He found that the notes produced by a string depend in a simple way on its length. If the length of the string is halved, the string produces a new, higher note that is harmonious with the original note. In fact, it is one octave above the original note. (The sequence of eight notes in the major scale, do, re, me, fa, so, la, te, do, cover one octave.) Harmonious notes are also produced when the string is stopped at two-thirds and four-fifths of its original length.

Another key feature of the strings in musical instruments is their weight. If two strings of the same length are stretched equally tightly, the heavier one will vibrate more slowly and give out a note of lower pitch. That is why the low-pitched strings of instruments are far thicker and heavier than the higher-pitched strings.

TRY THIS

Louder twang
Here is a way of demonstrating that solids conduct sounds better than air does.

What to do
First, stretch a rubber band with the finger and thumb of one hand and strum it. You can hear a faint twanging sound. Next, stretch the rubber band around a plastic glass (see the illustration). Place the base of the glass against your ear, and strum the band again. This time, it makes a much louder twang.

When a stretched string vibrates (on a violin or guitar, for example), it produces sound. When you strummed the rubber band stretched with your fingers, the slight sound it made traveled through the air to your ears. But when you stretched the band around the plastic glass and then strummed it, the sound was carried to your ear through the plastic. Because plastic is a solid, it conducts sound much better than air does. (Actually, the sound is also amplified a little by the hollow formed by the glass, which acts rather like the hollow body of an acoustic guitar or violin.)

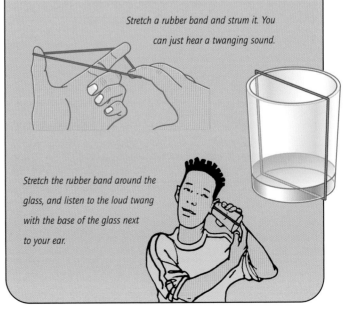

Stretch a rubber band and strum it. You can just hear a twanging sound.

Stretch the rubber band around the glass, and listen to the loud twang with the base of the glass next to your ear.

VIBRATING COLUMNS OF AIR

Organs, trumpets, flutes, and the human voice have something in common: they make sound because a volume of air is vibrating inside them, not something solid. The job of the player—or speaker—is to control the amount of air that vibrates at each moment.

Most of the sounds that we hear have been caused by something solid vibrating and setting up vibrations in the air. But it is also possible for a quantity of air trapped inside some kind of enclosure to vibrate, causing vibrations in the air outside the enclosure that spread out freely as sound waves. An easy way to make this happen is to blow across the mouth of a bottle. When you blow at the correct angle, you will produce a loud, musical note that is made by the air inside the bottle vibrating.

You can "tune" the bottle to make notes of a different pitch by pouring in water. The new note will be higher than the first one because the amount of air inside is less. You can set up a number of bottles tuned to different notes in this way and play tunes on them.

The same principle is used in wind instruments. The air in the pipe or tube of the instrument vibrates to make the sound. The longer the column of air that vibrates, the deeper the note.

Organs consist of a set of pipes, each playing a single note. Air is blown into them mechanically. The organist uses hands and feet to press keys that allow air into whichever pipes are needed at each moment.

In some organ pipes, called flue pipes, the air passes in through a specially shaped inlet that sets up the vibration. In others, called reed pipes, the air passes over a piece of flexible metal called a reed, and it is this that vibrates, setting the air in the pipe vibrating. Similar sorts of air inlet appear in other types of wind instrument.

One of the simplest of all wind instruments is the penny whistle. It is basically a tube with a shaped mouthpiece, called a fipple. The tube is open at the other end, too. There is a series of holes along the pipe. By closing the holes with his or her fingers, the player alters the effective length of the pipe and thus the pitch of the sound.

Nodes and antinodes

The pitch or frequency of the sound made by a vibrating column of air depends on its wavelength. The

WOODWIND INSTRUMENTS

In the recorder and penny whistle, two members of the flute family, the player closes holes with the fingers while blowing into the mouthpiece. Waves are set up with nodes at the closed holes, and this determines the pitch of the note that is produced (here all the holes are closed).

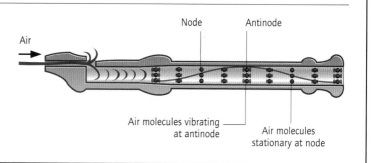

Air · Node · Antinode · Air molecules vibrating at antinode · Air molecules stationary at node

38

Brass players make their lips vibrate as they blow, so making the air in the instrument vibrate. They alter the length of the vibrating column of air by moving valves that alter the effective length of the airway in the instrument.

wavelength of a vibration is related to the distance from one node (a place where there is no vibration) to the next, or from one antinode (a place where there is maximum vibration) to the next. Opening and closing holes in a musical instrument alters the positions of antinodes, thus affecting the wavelength of the vibrations and the frequency of the sound.

Woodwind and brass

Both the recorder and the flute are fundamentally the same kind of instrument as the penny whistle. Clarinets and saxophones differ in having a reed to provide the vibration; oboes and bassoons have a pair of reeds that vibrate against each other. All of these instruments are known as woodwind because originally they were made of wood.

TRY THIS

Pipes of Pan
Another way of producing sound is to make a column of air vibrate inside a tube or a pipe (as in a recorder or penny whistle, for example). The pitch of the note—how high or low it sounds—depends on the width of the pipe and its length. In this project, you will make a set of musical pipes.

What to do
Stick several strips of double-sided tape to a piece of cardboard about 6 in (15 cm) square. Stick a dozen drinking straws to the tape in a row side by side, with the ends of the straws lined up along one edge of the card. Then cut through the other ends of the straws, and the cardboard, at an angle (see the illustration). Hold the tops of the straws near your bottom lip, and blow across and down. After a little practice, you will be able to get the straws to make sounds.

By blowing across the ends of the straws, you made the air inside them vibrate. This produced the sounds. Notice that the short straws produce higher-pitched notes than the longer straws. The ancient Greeks made a musical instrument of graduated pipes, which they called a panpipe, after Pan, the god of flocks and fields. Native South Americans still play panpipes today.

Stick straws to the cardboard, cut through at an angle, and then play the panpipes.

VIBRATING SKINS AND SOLIDS

The first primitive music apart from song must have been the bangs and crashes made by knocking objects together. Since then percussion instruments have been developed into sophisticated devices. Percussion plays a major role in serious music and often dominates rock and pop.

When you tap two pebbles together, you are unlikely to hear anything that is more interesting than a dull click. Hollow objects generally make louder and more musical notes than solid ones. This fact is used by detectives and customs officials when they tap the bottom of a suitcase to see whether there is a hollow inside it in which something could be hidden and smuggled into the country.

THE GLOCKENSPIEL

The glockenspiel consists of metal bars tuned a half-note apart. They are arranged like the keys of a piano, with the bars corresponding to the black piano keys in the upper row. Letters are note names.

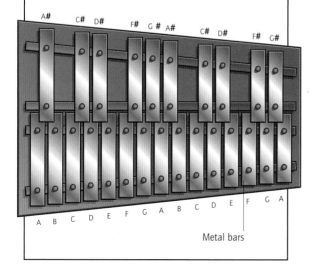

A# C# D# F# G# A# C# D# F# G#

A B C D E F G A B C D E F G A

Metal bars

A hollow log can make a booming noise. Dried seed-cases or gourds (a type of large, hollow fruit) make sharp, distinctive noises when tapped. There were enough musical-sounding natural objects to give our prehistoric ancestors the idea of shaping solid objects to form musical instruments.

The xylophone

A xylophone consists of wooden bars cut to precise lengths to give the desired notes when struck. Smaller bars make higher notes. An array of these bars mounted on a frame makes an instrument with a wide range of frequencies. Hollow gourds, again of carefully chosen sizes, may be hung beneath the bars to amplify the sound. In the modern xylophone metal tubes are often used as resonators.

In a vibraphone, the keys are made of metal (aluminum), with tubular metal resonators mounted beneath the keys to amplify the sound. Rotating disks within the resonators cause the pitch of each note to oscillate slightly.

Drums

In the same way that a stretched string produces a musical note when it is plucked (see page 36), so a taut skin or other membrane makes a note when it is struck. If the skin is stretched over a hollow vessel, a loud, pleasing noise is produced. In many types of drum there is a mixture of many frequencies in the note, which does not have the pure sound of a plucked string. But some drums, such as the steel drums made from oil containers and widely played in the Caribbean region, are designed to be tuned precisely.

TRY THIS

Noisy ruler

A xylophone is a percussion instrument that makes use of vibrating strips of wood. In this project, you will use a vibrating ruler to produce sounds.

What to do

First, clamp the ruler to the table with your hand, with part of the ruler projecting over the edge. With your other hand, twang the free end of the ruler (by pressing it down with a finger and releasing it suddenly). Try it several times with different lengths of ruler projecting. Which makes the highest note, a short length or a long length?

For a different type of sound, press the ruler against the table with most of its length projecting over the edge. Twang it as before, but this time quickly slide the ruler farther onto the table.

The pitch of the note (whether it is high or low) depends on the length of ruler that is vibrating. The shorter the length, the higher the note. When you slid the vibrating ruler farther onto the table, you continuously changed the length from long to short. As a result, the note changed pitch from low to high.

The pitch of the note depends on the length of the twanging ruler.

Twang the ruler, and slide it back to shorten the overhanging length.

TRY THIS

Ringing spoons

By now you will be used to the idea that vibrating objects produce sounds, and that sounds travel through materials. In this project, you will make ordinary spoons chime like church bells.

What to do

Tie the handle of a teaspoon at the center of a piece of string about 4 ft (1.3 m) long. Wind the ends of the string around your index fingers, keeping both halves of the string the same length. Place the tips of your fingers in your ears (do not push them in too far!). Lean forward so that the spoon hangs free, and let it hit the leg of a chair or a table (or get a friend to hit it with a wooden spoon). You will hear a chiming sound like a church bell. Repeat the procedure with larger spoons. What happens to the pitch of the sounds—are they higher or lower?

The sounds come from the vibrating spoons, and the string carries the sounds right into your ears. The larger the spoon, the lower the tone of its chime. You can make the sounds even louder by passing the ends of the string through holes in the bases of paper or Styrofoam cups. Tie a knot on the inside of the cup, or tape the string into place. Put the open ends of the cups over your ears, and ring those chimes!

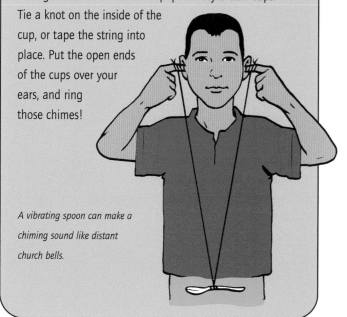

A vibrating spoon can make a chiming sound like distant church bells.

Keeping up the tension

The note made by a drum depends not only on its size, but also on the tension—the tautness—of the skin. The tighter the skin is, the higher the note. One traditional type of drum used in Africa and elsewhere has skin stretched over both ends by cords. The drum body has a "waist" so that the strings are clear of the body. The player holds the drum under one arm and squeezes the cage of cords while beating the drum with the other hand, creating a varying pitch.

A symphony orchestra usually has four or more tunable drums called kettledrums (or timpani). Originally the drum's skin was tightened (to raise the pitch of the note) or slackened (to lower the note) by turning keys

A rock drummer playing a drum kit consisting of several types of drum and cymbal. Their sounds fall into different ranges, and they can have different qualities or "colors" of sound according to the way in which they are struck.

PERCUSSION INSTRUMENTS

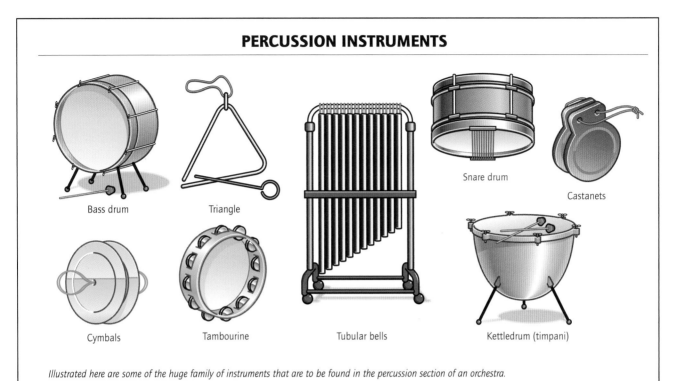

Bass drum

Triangle

Snare drum

Castanets

Cymbals

Tambourine

Tubular bells

Kettledrum (timpani)

Illustrated here are some of the huge family of instruments that are to be found in the percussion section of an orchestra.

mounted around the rim. In more modern kettledrums a foot pedal is used to stretch or slacken the skin.

Bells, gongs, and cymbals

Metals make a satisfying clang when struck. That is because they have a polycrystalline structure built from lattices of atoms that vibrate with very precise frequencies when they are hit. A maintenance engineer can judge the condition of a wheel on a train by hitting it with a hammer. A good wheel will produce a musical note, but a cracked wheel will make a dull, flat sound.

Most bells are made of metal. The largest musical instruments of all are mighty church bells, made of bronze and weighing over 10 tons.

Priests at some temples in Asia call worshippers to prayer by striking large gongs. These gongs are usually cast or beaten out of bronze. Unlike a bell, a gong does not have a definite pitch, but produces a mixture of tones. A cymbal is similar, but is made from a disk of brass. Cymbals are often played in pairs to produce a metallic crashing sound when they are struck together.

SPEED OF SOUND

The fact that sound travels at a definite speed is easily noticed. The speed varies according to the medium in which the sound travels. Sound waves can be outpaced by jet planes, by space rockets during launch, and now even by jet-propelled cars.

Picture yourself in the middle of a thunderstorm. You see a lightning stroke 3 miles (5 km) away. The light reaches you almost instantly—after about 1/60,000 of a second. But the sound, traveling at a speed of 1 mile every 5 seconds (1 kilometer every 3 seconds), takes 15 seconds to arrive.

You can see a delay even over shorter distances. The sound of a hammer blow 330 feet (100 meters) away is delayed by a noticeable one-third of a second from the sight of the hammer falling. (You never see this in movies. Directors always arrange for the boom of a distant explosion to coincide with the sight of it. They think their audience will be puzzled by a delay!)

SCIENCE WORDS

- **Doppler effect:** The change in frequency of a wave caused by the relative motion of the source and the observer. For example, the pitch of an ambulance siren seems to fall as the vehicle passes, then recedes from a listener.
- **Mach number:** The ratio of the speed of an object to the speed of sound.
- **Shock wave:** A disturbance that moves through a fluid, such as air or water, faster than the speed of sound in that fluid.
- **Sonic boom:** An explosive sound caused by the shock wave preceding an aircraft traveling at or above the speed of sound.

The speed of sound in air increases with increases in temperature. At 32°F (0°C) it is 1,088 feet per second (331.6 meters per second) in dry air. At 68°F (20°C) it is 1,129 ft/s (344 m/s). The temperature of the atmosphere decreases up to an altitude of about 8 miles (13 km), and so does the speed of sound. At this height the speed of sound falls to about 938 ft/s (286 m/s).

Mach number

The ratio of the speed of an object to the speed of sound under the same circumstances is called its Mach number. Mach 1 is the speed of sound, Mach 2 is twice the speed of sound, and so on. The Mach number is

F-18 Hornet fighters of the US Navy breaking the sound barrier. Objects traveling faster than the speed of sound form a conically shaped high pressure surface, clearly seen around the lead airplane, and generate a shock wave and sonic boom. This cone is caused by the sound source (the jet) traveling faster than the sound waves produced by it. High humidity levels make the cone visible.

named after the Austrian physicist Ernst Mach (1838-1916).

Sound waves travel faster through liquids and solids. At sea a distant explosion will be heard twice—the first sound has traveled through water, and the second sound has traveled through air. The speed of sound in water is about four and a half times its speed in air.

DOPPLER EFFECT

As a police car speeds toward a listening bystander, each sound wave has a shorter distance to travel to the listener than the previous one. The frequency is raised, and the sound rises in pitch. When the police car has passed by and is speeding away, the sound waves are stretched, their frequency is lowered, and the pitch of the siren falls.

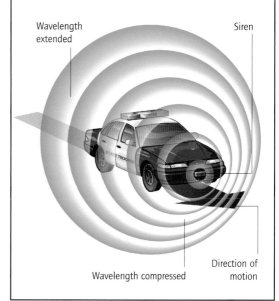

Wavelength extended

Siren

Wavelength compressed

Direction of motion

Christian Doppler

The Austrian scientist Christian Doppler (1803-1853) showed how apparent frequency and wavelength vary according to the motion of the source and the listener. When the source of the waves is approaching the listener, or vice versa, the apparent frequency increases. If the source and the listener are moving apart, the apparent frequency is lowered. In 1845, Doppler ran an experiment to demonstrate this effect. A locomotive pulled a carriage of trumpeters past other musicians, who judged the change in pitch of the notes as the train went past. Their judgments matched his predictions.

SUPERSONIC AND SUBSONIC VIBRATIONS

We are surrounded by ultrasound—sound so high-pitched that we cannot hear it. But animals can make these sounds and respond to them, and they fill the air and oceans with unheard cries. We make use of ultrasound in industry, warfare, and medicine.

The deepest sounds we can hear consist of about 20 vibrations per second, or 20 hertz—named for the German physicist Heinrich Hertz (1857-1894); its symbol is Hz. The highest audible frequency is about 20,000 Hz, or 20 kilohertz (1 kilohertz, symbol kHz, is 1,000 hertz).

Sound waves with frequencies higher than this are called "ultrasonic" or "supersonic." (This has nothing to do with supersonic speed: the speed of these waves is the same as that of sound with lower frequencies.)

Many animals are able to hear this ultrasound. Dog whistles produce loud ultrasound, which dogs react to but which people cannot hear. Bats have an uncanny ability to find their way and hunt prey in darkness. They give out high-pitched squeaks at ultrasonic frequencies that can be as high as 200 kHz, and they detect the echoes from insects and other objects.

Producing ultrasound

The usual way of producing audible sound is through a loudspeaker, in which a paper or metal diaphragm vibrates rapidly to create the sounds. But a diaphragm cannot be made to vibrate fast enough to produce ultrasound. Instead, the sound producer—called a transducer—employs a crystal that is made to vibrate by an oscillating electric current applied across its faces. The crystal is usually made of quartz or a chemical called Rochelle salt. Ultrasound produced in this way is used for cleaning things. For example,

Ultrasound can be used to look into the body. Here a human fetus is seen in the womb. Ultrasound scans are routine during pregnancy.

clothing can be submerged in water or cleaning fluid and rapidly agitated to remove dirt by beaming in an ultrasound signal.

Undersea sound

The bats' method of navigation is used by seafarers. Ultrasonic pulses sent out from ships are reflected from, for example, submarines, shoals of fish, or the seabed. The time the echo takes to return to the ship shows the distance of the object.

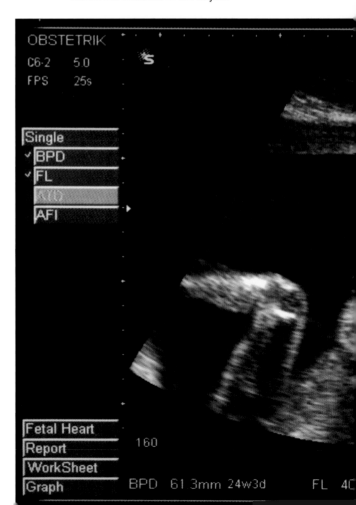

Now sonar is used in medicine. Ultrasound pulses can penetrate the human body, and the echoes from internal organs paint a picture of the body's interior.

The deep, low-frequency sounds from a church organ, or from a truck or plane, can make an entire building throb. In these cases, as well as the sounds we can hear there are vibrations that are of lower frequency. These vibrations are called infrasound, or subsonic sound. Although human beings cannot hear infrasound, many animals can, among them whales and elephants.

Lower-frequency sounds travel farther than higher-frequency ones. That is why distant thunder is always deep and rumbling, while a nearby thunderclap is much sharper, with a cracking tone to it. Some animals take advantage of the long range of low-frequency sound. Whales emit infrasound to communicate over distances of as much as 100 miles (160 km).

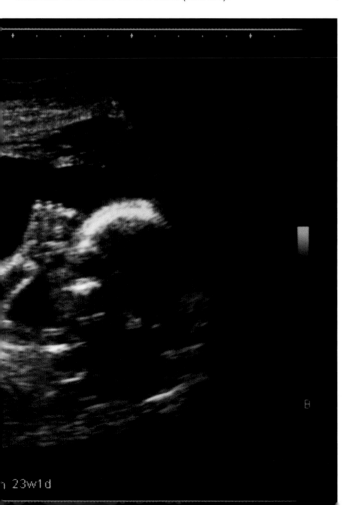

HUNTING WITH ULTRASOUND

Bats navigate using high-frequency sound as sonar. Most of the sound they produce is too high-pitched for us to hear. The bats' large and sensitive ears detect echoes, enabling the bats to home in on insects and avoid obstacles. So amazingly accurate is their navigational ability that bats can fly safely through darkened rooms criss-crossed by wires.

In the 1980s, naturalists discovered that elephants produce subsonic rumbling noises from their nasal passages. They use these sounds to communicate with one another over long distances.

Sound and movement

The throbbing that a deep sound makes is caused by a phenomenon called resonance. An object is said to resonate when it is made to vibrate by the vibration of some other nearby object. For example, sounding a single note near a piano—by plucking a guitar string, say—will cause the piano string that is tuned to the same note to vibrate. Other strings, such as those an octave higher or lower, will do the same.

The vibrations of the air from the plucked string tend to make all the piano strings vibrate, but only those piano strings that naturally vibrate at the same frequency as the guitar string will develop a strong vibration. In a similar way, if someone pushing a child on a playground swing gives little pushes at just the same rate that the child is swinging, the movement of the swing will build up. Pushes at a different rate will be out of step with the regular motion of the swing, and this motion will be prevented from building up.

Buildings and furniture do not usually resonate to normal sound frequencies. Because the natural rates of vibration of these objects are low, they resonate (if they resonate at all) to infrasound. Over time a concert hall or church can be damaged by deep notes from an organ.

A spectacular example of harmful resonance occurred in 1940, when the wind caused the Tacoma Narrows suspension bridge in Washington to vibrate uncontrollably. The deck of the bridge snaked like a shaken rope, flinging cars into the river below and finally collapsing. Since that disaster new bridges have always incorporated antiresonance features.

The shaking Earth

Most earthquakes are caused by shifts within the top 190 miles (about 300 km) of the Earth's mantle. The shifts are small, but affect enormous quantities of rock. The shifts cause vibrations of all frequencies in the

Charles Richter

US seismologist Charles Richter (1900-1985) will always be associated with the earthquake scale named after him. He devised it with another seismologist, Beno Gutenberg (1889-1960), in 1927-1935. They rated the amount of energy released in an earthquake by the size of the marks made by the pen of a seismograph, with a correction for the distance of the earthquake from the observing laboratory. The points on the scale do not represent equal intervals. When you go from one point on the scale to the next, the energy released in the earthquake is multiplied by about 30.

surrounding crust. Some vibrations travel for large distances through the crust, others through the deeper parts of the Earth—the mantle and core. Earthquake vibrations are the sound of a whole planet being shaken.

Shear waves and pressure waves

Sound waves in a solid, unlike sound waves in a fluid such as water or air, can be of two kinds. In one, atoms and molecules are made to vibrate backward and

RICHTER SCALE

The energy released in an earthquake is described by the numbers on the Richter scale. The amount of damage caused by the earthquake depends not only on its magnitude on the Richter scale, but also on its depth and on the numbers of people and buildings in the area. Another scale, the Mercalli scale, rates earthquakes according to their visible effects.

2.5 Not generally felt, but recorded on seismometers
3.5 Felt by many people
5.0 Some local damage
7.5 Destructive earthquake
8.5 Major earthquake

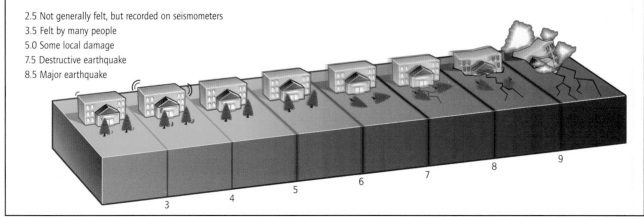

forward in the same direction as the motion of the wave. This is the same as the movement of the particles in a sound wave in a gas or liquid. But in the other kind of sound wave in a solid, the atoms or molecules move from side to side. These waves are like the waves you can send along a rope that is fixed at one end by shaking its free end.

In the study of earthquakes, the side-to-side waves are called S (shear) waves, and the faster, pressure waves are called P waves. The different conditions of pressure, density, and rock composition at different depths below the surface of the Earth affect the speeds of both S waves and P waves.

The varying conditions in the body of the planet cause the paths of earthquake waves (known as seismic waves) to bend. The pattern of waves arriving at different places around the world following an earthquake is very complex, but over many years they have been disentangled to reveal a lot about the structure of the Earth. They reveal a difference between the lighter rocks of the thin crust and the denser rocks of the mantle, which extends halfway toward the center. And they show that there is a liquid core of molten iron and nickel that the S waves cannot penetrate. There is also an innermost solid iron–nickel core.

When a tremor is felt in a particular spot, the ground generally moves both from side to side and up and down. Seismographs, or Earth-tremor measuring devices, record these tremors as graphs, traditionally on paper. The instrument consists of a pendulum, which has a heavy weight or bob, that is free either to bounce up and down on a spring or to swing from side to side. The bob carries a pen that makes a trace on paper mounted on a revolving drum. The heavy bob tends to stay still, while the rest of the instrument shakes during a tremor, producing the wavy trace. Nowadays the information is often recorded electronically as computer data rather than as an ink trace.

This sort of damage can be caused by an earthquake that shakes the ground for only a few moments and makes it move only a few inches.

REFLECTION AND REFRACTION OF SOUND

Even in total darkness we can sense the presence of objects around us. This ability is largely due to our subconscious perceptions of sounds reflected by objects. The principle of reflection of sound is used in sonar to detect objects under water.

Sound waves, like all other types of wave, can be reflected. They can be reflected by solid objects, by the surface of water, and even by the boundary between layers of water that are at different temperatures beneath the surface. A reflected sound is called an echo.

An echo from a distant object is noticeably delayed compared with the original sound. When you shout or clap your hands to hear the echo, every 5 seconds' delay represents 1 mile (3 seconds' delay represents 1 kilometer). To figure out the distance of the object that is reflecting the sound, you have to divide the delay time by two, because the sound has traveled both ways by the time you hear the echo.

Echoes all around

Echoes from nearby objects are not obvious, but they do affect the quality of all the sounds we hear. A radio program made in the open air sounds quite different from one made indoors, where there are echoes from walls and ceilings. The sounds in a huge cathedral are very different from those in a small kitchen. A room

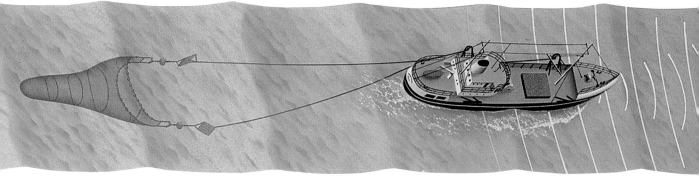

A military helicopter lowering a side-scanning sonar buoy into the ocean. Devices such as this send out pulses that bounce off the sea bottom and can detect hazardous underwater obstacles like wrecks, or the presence of explosive mines.

echoes when it is empty of people and of soft furnishings, such as drapes and upholstered chairs, which absorb a great deal of the sound. The characteristics of the sound inside a room or building are called its acoustics.

Multiple echoes can be confusing. For example, somebody listening to a speaker but sitting toward the back of a large hall hears sounds coming to them by several routes, but not all at exactly the same time. In addition to the sound of the speaker's voice arriving directly, sounds also arrive a fraction of a second later after having been reflected from the walls and from the ceiling. This mixture of sounds distorts the speaker's voice. Such reflections can be avoided by covering the walls and ceilings with sound-absorbent materials, such as tiles made from foamed plastics.

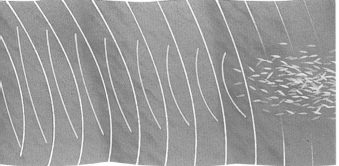

Sonar is of huge importance to the fishing industry. Even small fishing vessels search for shoals of fish with sonar. From the trace on the sonar screen, an experienced operator can judge the size of the shoal and can often tell what type of fish it is.

In a well-designed theater or concert hall the tip-up seats absorb about the same amount of sound as a person sitting in them. As a result, the hall has the same acoustic properties even if many of the seats are empty.

Refraction of sound

The paths of sound waves can be gently bent as well as sharply reflected. Sound waves, like other waves, usually bend when their speed changes.

For example, sound slows down when it enters cooler air. Normally, air high up is cooler than air near the ground. Sound waves rising at an angle to the horizontal from a source on the ground are slowed as they rise. The braking effect drags them around so that they are bent upward. (This is rather like a column of soldiers marching at an angle onto rough ground that slows them down. They tend to deviate from the direction they were marching in.)

This bending upward tends to reduce the loudness of the sound at ground level some distance from the

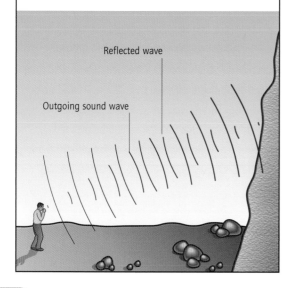

MAKING ECHOES

You hear an echo of your own voice when some of its sound energy is reflected from an object and returned to you. A rocky cliff or the wall of a building make good echoes.

Reflected wave

Outgoing sound wave

---

source. In the open air, sounds are weaker at a distance than they would be in air of uniform temperature.

The effects can be the reverse when air is warmer higher up than it is near the ground. This happens in certain weather conditions and is common in the polar regions, where the air is chilled near the frozen ground. Sound waves are speeded up as they rise, and this makes them swerve downward. It is then often possible to hear quiet sounds over great distances.

Blowing in the wind

The wind also affects audibility for a similar reason. Windspeed normally increases with height, and the

Loudspeaker horns on a public address system. Their shape helps concentrate the sound waves that they emit into a narrow beam. In foggy conditions, banks of loudspeakers at coastguard stations send a powerful blast of sound far out to sea to warn passing ships that they are near the shore .

effect of this is to make any sound waves traveling upwind bend upward, and any sound waves traveling downwind bend downward. This makes it easier to hear people speaking, for example, when they are standing upwind of you (see illustration right).

Sounds can be made easier to hear if they are focused into a beam. They are stronger within the beam and weaker anywhere outside the beam. A loudspeaker, an old-fashioned phonograph, and a loudhailer all have a horn whose shape is designed to reflect sound waves into a limited beam, rather than spreading them outward in all directions.

SCIENCE WORDS

- **Amplifier:** A device that increases the strength of a sound or of an electronic signal representing a sound, as in a radio or hi-fi.
- **Beam:** A concentrated stream of particles or a similar configuration of light or sound waves.
- **Downwind:** In the same direction toward which the wind is blowing, that is, with the wind from behind.
- **Upwind:** In or toward the direction from which the wind is blowing.

HEARING AND THE WIND

Windspeed usually increases with height. Higher above the ground sound waves going upwind are slowed down. All the sound waves going in that direction are therefore bent upward. They are hard to hear at ground level. Higher-altitude sound waves going downwind are speeded up and bent downward, making them easier to hear.

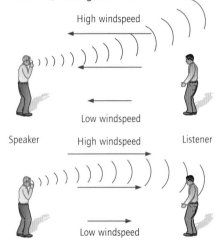

High windspeed

Low windspeed

Speaker   High windspeed   Listener

Low windspeed

HORN OF PLENTY

The earliest record-players, or phonographs, did not have electronic amplifiers and loudspeakers. Sound was generated directly by the vibration of the needle as it moved in the record groove. A large horn amplified the faint sound and directed it toward the listener.

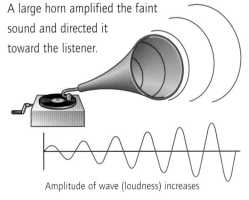

Amplitude of wave (loudness) increases

THE HUMAN EAR

Our ears give us knowledge of the world of sounds around us. The complex analysis of sounds, telling us what frequencies are present in them, takes place in hidden structures within the head. Our sense of balance is located in the same structures. Most defects of hearing, apart from total deafness, can be corrected by physicians.

Human beings detect sound by means of a marvelously complex sensory mechanism. The visible flaps of skin that we call ears, and anatomists call pinnas or pinnae, are only the outermost part of a structure that goes deep into the head. This structure is divided into the outer, middle, and inner ears.

Sounds from the outside world pass down a passage called the auditory canal and make the eardrum

We can keep our balance, sense which way up we are, and judge how our body is moving thanks to the semicircular canals, organs in the inner ear.

SCIENCE WORDS

- **Auditory canal:** The passage that runs from the visible ear, or pinna, into the head.
- **Cochlea:** A spiral organ in the inner ear that contains fluid and has many nerves attached. It is responsible for the detection of sounds.
- **Eardrum:** Also called tympanum, a membrane separating the outer ear from the middle ear. It vibrates when sound waves strike it, passing the vibrations to a chain of small linked bones in the middle ear.
- **Inner ear:** The part of the ear that contains the organs of hearing and balance. See also Cochlea; Semicircular canals.
- **Semicircular canals:** Loop-shaped, fluid-filled organs in the inner ear that provide the sense of balance.

vibrate (see the illustration on the opposite page). These vibrations are passed through a chain of three small bones to a complicated fluid-filled structure in the inner ear called the cochlea. The vibrations of the fluid in turn cause small, fine cells called hair cells to vibrate, generating electrical signals. The signals travel to the brain, and a sound is perceived. The deepest, longest-wavelength sounds travel farthest along the cochlea; so when hairs in that far part of the cochlea vibrate, the brain can "work out" that there are low frequencies in the sound that has been heard.

Achieving balance

Our sense of balance is also controlled from the inner ear, where there are three fluid-filled loops called the semicircular canals at right angles to one another. Movements of the head set the fluid in the canals in motion, providing information from which the brain

can compute the position
and movement of the head in
relation to the direction of gravity.
Giddiness is caused by the fluid in the canals
continuing to move after the head has stopped moving.

Hearing problems

Various things can upset the delicate hearing mechanism,
with results that vary from hardness of hearing to
profound deafness. The simplest cause of partial
deafness is an obstruction in the auditory canal, most
often by earwax, which is easily removed. Inflammation
of the middle ear (otitis) is another possible cause that
can usually be treated successfully. More difficult to
remedy are problems with the ear's sound-detecting
apparatus, the auditory nerve, or the brain's hearing
center. A hearing aid may help; an alternative is a
cochlear implant, in which audio signals are fed to an
electrode placed in the inner ear.

*Tuning forks like the one being used here by a piano tuner give out
a pure tone of a single frequency. Such sounds are almost unknown
in nature.*

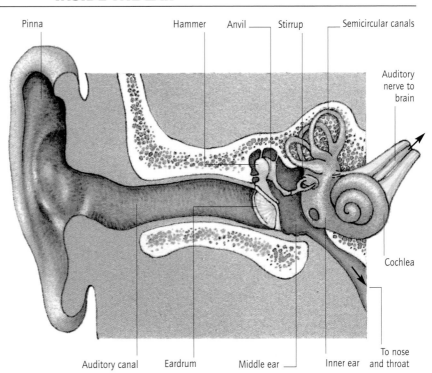

INSIDE THE EAR

The pinna, or ear-flap, is shaped
to give us information about the
direction from which a sound comes.
Sound waves are channeled along
the auditory canal, making the
eardrum vibrate. Beyond the eardrum
is the middle ear, which is connected
to the nose and throat. The vibrations
of the eardrum are passed along
three bones joined together, called
the hammer (malleus), anvil (incus),
and stirrup (stapes). The movement
of the stirrup sets up vibrations in the
fluid-filled inner ear. Hairlike cells in
the coiled tube of the cochlea send
electrical signals to the brain. The
three fluid-filled semicircular canals
detect head movements.

Pinna · Hammer · Anvil · Stirrup · Semicircular canals · Auditory nerve to brain · Cochlea · Auditory canal · Eardrum · Middle ear · Inner ear · To nose and throat

THE HUMAN VOICE

The human voice is astonishingly complex and flexible. Subtle, controlled movements of the jaws, tongue, lips, teeth, and vocal cords together produce the countless different types of vocal sound. Children master this control in the first few years of life, but scientists are still patiently uncovering the intricacies of human speech.

Whenever we shout, speak, sing, or whistle our vocals cords—which are relaxed when we are simply breathing—come together.

The human voice works like a combination of a wind instrument and a stringed instrument. It is produced by air from the lungs blowing between two organs called the vocal cords. They are housed in the larynx, or voicebox, which lies at the front of the throat and at the top of the windpipe, or trachea (see opposite).

The vocal cords form a V shape across the windpipe. They are made of elastic tissue and can be pulled by muscles in the larynx. When the muscles are relaxed, the vocal cords are relatively far apart, and no sound is made by air passing through. The muscles can move the cords together, and then they vibrate as air passes

between them. The muscles can also tighten the cords, raising the pitch, or loosen them to lower the pitch.

At puberty there are changes in the larynx. Boys' vocal cords generally become less tightly stretched, so that the pitch of the voice drops.

The epiglottis is part of the larynx. This flap of cartilage closes off the top of the windpipe when we

---

SHAPING SOUNDS

Mouth movements that produce some of the consonant sounds are shown here. B and P, for example, are called plosive because the lips are pressed together and then parted, releasing air explosively. T and D are called alveolar, because the tongue is briefly pressed against the alveolus, the front of the roof of the mouth. Other sounds have different classifications.

B and P

T and D

F and V

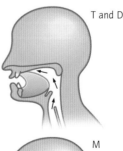

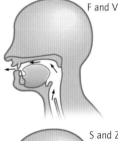

R

M

S and Z

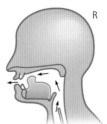

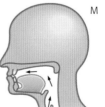

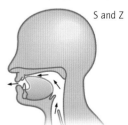

swallow so that food cannot enter the windpipe and perhaps choke us. The food is diverted into the esophagus, or gullet, the tube that leads to the stomach.

Voiced and unvoiced sounds

Some sounds are made without the vocal cords vibrating. They are called unvoiced, and include the P and T sounds. The B and D sounds, by contrast, are made with vibration of the vocal cords and are described as voiced. Voiced sounds also include all the vowels.

The sounds generated in the larynx are modified in the mouth. We make complex movements of the tongue, lips, and teeth to form the vowel and consonant sounds of speech. Tongue and lip positions are shown for some consonants in the diagram below left.

There is a wide range of frequencies in human speech. The ability to detect high frequencies is important in distinguishing many of the consonants from one another. The commonest forms of deafness that develop as people get older involve difficulty in distinguishing sounds in this way.

Voiceprints

There are individual differences in the mix of frequencies in different people's voices, even when speaking the same words. These frequencies can be electronically analyzed and represented in an image called a voiceprint. A voiceprint can be used to identify the speaker with the same certainty with which a fingerprint can identify an individual. A recording of a nuisance telephone call can be turned into a voiceprint that can be compared with the voiceprint of a suspect.

SCIENCE WORDS

● **Larynx:** Also called the voicebox, the organ in the human throat that contains the vocal cords.
● **Vocal cords:** The elastic organs in the throat that produce the human voice by vibrating as air is expelled between them.

MACHINERY OF SPEECH

The vocal cords are housed in a container called the larynx, at the top of the windpipe, or trachea, which lies at the front of the throat. When speaking, a person blows air through the vocal cords while altering their position and tension to vary the pitch of the sounds produced. Movements of the mouth make further alterations in the sounds to produce recognizable speech.

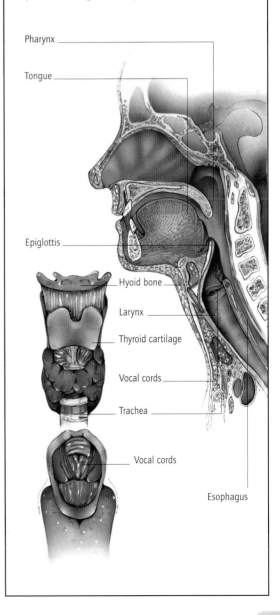

Pharynx

Tongue

Epiglottis

Hyoid bone

Larynx

Thyroid cartilage

Vocal cords

Trachea

Vocal cords

Esophagus

SOUND RECORDING AND REPRODUCTION

Nothing seems more elusive than a sound, which vanishes in a moment. Yet we have learned to store sounds, send them around the world, make them loud or soft at will, and mold them as if they were clay. With modern technology the vocal and instrumental sounds made by performers are now just raw material for the sound engineer.

The first sound recordings consisted of grooves in a wax surface whose shape was a direct imitation of the shape of waves of sound. They were made in 1877 by the American inventor Thomas Alva Edison (1847–1931), using his phonograph. A person would speak or sing loudly in front of the large end of a horn, and the sound was focused to make a metal plate vibrate. A needle attached to the plate cut a wavy groove into the soft surface of a revolving wax-coated cylinder.

To play back the sound, practically the same equipment was used in reverse. The cylinder rotated, making a needle in the groove vibrate. The needle was

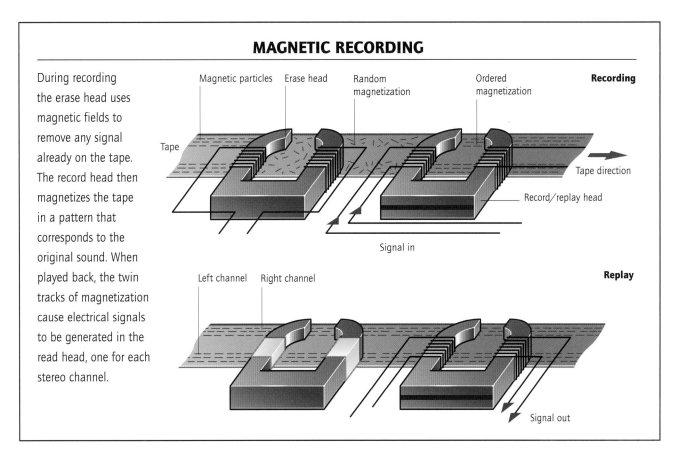

MAGNETIC RECORDING

Recording

During recording the erase head uses magnetic fields to remove any signal already on the tape. The record head then magnetizes the tape in a pattern that corresponds to the original sound. When played back, the twin tracks of magnetization cause electrical signals to be generated in the read head, one for each stereo channel.

Magnetic particles | Erase head | Random magnetization | Ordered magnetization

Tape

Tape direction

Record/replay head

Signal in

Replay

Left channel | Right channel

Signal out

---

attached to a plate, which also vibrated, reproducing a faint version of the original sound, which was amplified by a large horn.

Disks were soon found to be more convenient than cylinders. The first 78 rpm records were made from a type of resin called shellac. Vinyl, a type of plastic, was used for 33 and 45 rpm records from the 1950s onward.

Electronic recording

Sound recording was much improved when electronic microphones and loudspeakers were developed. Electronic microphones generate electric currents varying in strength, representing the varying intensity (loudness) of the sound from moment to moment. This signal controls the cutting of the original disk.

From the 1980s, miniaturization made it possible for people to listen to music on personal stereos. Earlier systems that used radios, cassette tapes, or CDs have now been replaced by digital music players.

When a vinyl disk is played back, the vibrations of the stylus (pickup head) are converted into an electric signal, which is used to drive a loudspeaker.

Magnetic recording

Recording on vinyl disks achieved superb quality, but was difficult to do outside the studio. Magnetic tape recording could be carried out to a reasonable standard by amateurs, and the equipment eventually became portable and convenient.

A magnetic recording tape consists of a plastic film coated with metallic particles. They become magnetized when exposed to a strong magnetic field. During recording the tape is wound past two electromagnets. An electromagnet consists of a wire carrying an electric current wrapped around a metal core. The current creates a magnetic field, which the metal core increases. So the whole device is a controllable magnet.

The first electromagnet in a tape recorder is called the erase head, and its job is to remove any existing magnetization on the tape. The second electromagnet is called the record/replay head. A varying current flows through it, representing the sound being recorded. This creates a varying magnetic field, and it in turn magnetizes the metal coating on the tape. A pattern of strong and weak magnetization is put onto the tape.

During playback the tape is wound past the record/playback head. The changing magnetic field generates a changing electrical signal in the head, which is converted into sound.

COMPACT DISK

In the underside of a CD, or compact disk, are etched billions of tiny pits, arranged in a spiral track. There are also regions, called flats, where there are no pits. The CD player's read head swings between the center and the edge of the disk as the disk spins. A laser beam (red) is shone onto the disk, and its reflections are sensed. The long sequence of pits and flats is thus translated into a stream of electronic signals. They in turn are converted into sound in the loudspeakers.

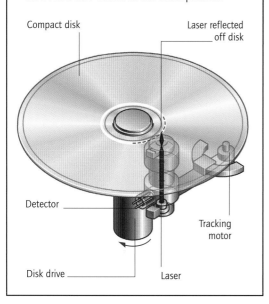

Compact disk

Laser reflected off disk

Detector

Tracking motor

Disk drive

Laser

Compact disks

The old-fashioned vinyl disk is an analog device: the wavy shape of the groove is just like a picture of the sound wave. In contrast, the compact disk, or CD, is a digital device, storing information about the sound in the form of a sequence of numbers (digits). It consists of a plastic-coated aluminum disk in which a track consisting of tiny pits about 0.6 of a micrometer (24 millionths of an inch) across spirals outward from the center.

At each position along the track a pit may be present or may be lacking. These two possibilities represent the two digits 0 and 1. Combinations of two digits are enough to represent any number in binary code.

A sound engineer at a mixing desk in the control room of a recording studio. Engineers use this equipment to mix dozens of tracks, each of them separate recordings of the session made by a different microphone.

Each group of 16 digits represents any number from 0 to 65,535. This corresponds to the loudness of the sound at any one moment. Just over 44,000 such groups stream from the CD pickup head every second (along with many more digits representing various kinds of error-checking and control information). Sampling a sound over 44,000 times per second is enough to represent it with an accuracy far surpassing what any other method of sound recording can achieve.

A new digital medium called MP3 was introduced in the 1990s. It compresses music by leaving out sounds that we do not normally hear, such as those above 16 kHz (the upper threshold of human hearing). MP3 is popular on the Internet since it enables tracks to be downloaded quickly.

TRY THIS

Paper amplifier

The first phonographs had a large metal horn to amplify the sound from the record. People also used to use horns—called megaphones—to amplify their voices. In this project, you will make such a horn and use it to listen to an unwanted record.

What to do

Cut two squares of strong paper, one about 6 in (15 cm) square, and the other twice as large. Form each piece of paper into a cone by rolling it from one corner and taping it together. Carefully push a steel pin crosswise through each cone near the pointed end so that the point of the pin sticks out. Put an unwanted record (a "45" would be ideal) on the turntable, and turn it on. Hold a cone lightly while placing the point of the pin in a groove on the record. Can you hear anything? Repeat the procedure with the other cone.

You should have heard music (or whatever else was on the record). The wavy groove in the record vibrates the pin, which in turn vibrates the paper horn. The vibration of the horn causes the air inside it to vibrate and produce sounds, all exactly in time with the sound vibrations represented on the record. The larger horn vibrates more air and produces louder sounds.

Roll the horns (a), tape them and add a pin (b), and place the pin in the record groove (c).

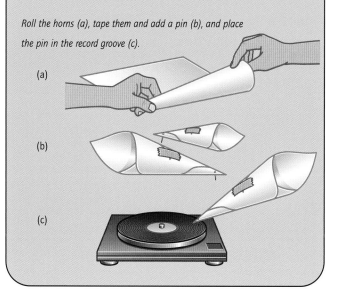

(a)

(b)

(c)

GLOSSARY

Acoustics 1. The science of sound. 2. The sound qualities of, for example a room, theater, or concert hall.

Amplifier A device that increases the strength of a sound or of an electronic signal representing a sound, as in a radio or hi-fi.

Amplitude The intensity of a wave. The amplitude of a sound wave is directly related to its loudness.

Analog Describing a signal or display that continuously varies. An analog signal resembles what it represents. For example, the groove on a traditional vinyl record is like a picture of the changing amplitude of the sound.

Angle of incidence The angle between an incident ray and the normal to a mirror or to the surface of a block of transparent material.

Angle of reflection The angle between the reflected ray and the normal to a mirror.

Antinode A position in a standing wave at which the amplitude is greatest.

CD Abbreviation for compact disk, a medium for recording sound, images, and data. It consists of a metal-coated plastic platter on which digital information is recorded as a track consisting of tiny pits.

Concave lens Also called a diverging lens, a type of lens that causes parallel rays of light to spread out (diverge) as if coming from a point (the focus) behind the lens. Its surfaces curve inward.

Concave mirror Also called a converging mirror, a type of mirror that causes parallel rays of light to be reflected to a focus in front of the mirror. Its surface curves inward.

Convex lens Also called a converging lens, a type of lens that causes parallel rays of light to converge to a point (the focus) in front of the lens. Its surfaces curve outward.

Convex mirror Also called a diverging mirror, a type of mirror that causes parallel rays of light to spread out (diverge) after reflection so that they appear to come from a point (the focus) behind the mirror. Its surface curves outward.

Decibel (dB) A unit of loudness equal to one tenth of a bel. If a sound is 10 dB louder than another one, it is 10 times as intense; if it is 20 dB louder, it is 10 * 10 = 100 times as intense, and so on.

Digital Describing a signal or display that uses digits (numerals) to represent something. For example, the display on a digital watch represents time as numbers rather than by the movement of hands.

Dispersion The splitting of white light into the colors of the rainbow (a spectrum), for example, by a triangular prism. Raindrops cause dispersion in a rainbow.

Doppler effect The change in frequency of a wave caused by the relative motion of the source and the observer. For example, the pitch of an ambulance siren seems to fall as the vehicle passes, then recedes from a listener.

Echolocation Finding the direction and distance of an object by beaming sound pulses at it and detecting the echoes. The technology used is called sonar.

Electron A subatomic particle with a negative electric charge. Electrons surround the nucleus of an atom. They play a key role in electricity, magnetism, and the conduction of heat.

Fluorescent bulb Also called a fluorescent tube, an electric lamp consisting of a tube containing mercury vapor, with electrodes at each end.

Frequency For a sound wave, the number of times per second that the air molecules (or the molecules of whatever material the wave is traveling through) vibrate.

Gravity The natural force of attraction exerted by the Earth, which draws bodies at or near its surface toward its center.

Incandescence The emission of light by an object that is heated to white heat.

Incandescent lamp An electric bulb that has a filament (usually made of tungsten) in a glass globe containing traces of an inert gas such as argon. The electric current heats the filament to incandescence.

Laws of reflection of light 1. The angle of incidence equals the angle of reflection. 2 The incident ray, the normal, and the reflected ray all lie in the same plane.

Lens A piece of transparent material that, by refraction, changes the direction of light rays passing through it.

Lunar eclipse An eclipse of the Moon, occurring when the Earth's shadow (cast by the Sun) falls onto the Moon.

Mach number The ratio of the speed of an object to the speed of sound.

Magnetic tape A plastic tape coated with a magnetic material that can record sounds and other forms of information. The strength of magnetization of the tape at each point represents the loudness of the sound at a particular moment.

Node A position in a standing wave at which the amplitude is zero (or smallest).

Photoelectric cell Also called a photocell, a current-producing device consisting of an element such as silicon that emits electrons when struck by light.

Prism A usually triangular block of a transparent material that can split white light into the colors of the rainbow.

Reflected ray A ray of light that is reflected by a mirror.

Refracted ray A ray of light that is refracted as it passes from one transparent material into another.

Refraction The bending of light rays as they pass from one transparent material into another.

Shock wave A disturbance that moves through a fluid, such as air or water, faster than the speed of sound in that fluid.

Solar eclipse An eclipse of the Sun, caused by the Moon passing between the Earth and the Sun.

Solar panel 1. A device consisting of hundreds of photoelectric cells used, for example, to provide the electric power for space probes. 2. A thin tank containing water and painted black. It absorbs the Sun's radiation, which heats the water.

Supersonic flow Flow of a fluid at more than the speed of sound in that fluid. It is marked by shock waves.

Ultrasound Sound of frequency too high to be heard by human beings.

Vacuum A completely empty space in which there are no atoms or molecules of any substance.

Wavelength The distance between two successive locations where a wave is at its maximum intensity.

FURTHER RESEARCH

Books – General

Bloomfield, Louis A. *How Things Work: The Physics of Everyday Life.* Hoboken, NJ: Wiley, 2009.

Bloomfield, Louis A. *How Everything Works: Making Physics Out of the Ordinary.* Hoboken, NJ: Wiley, 2007.

Challoner, Jack. *Eyewitness Visual Dictionary of Physics.* New York, NY: DK Publishing, 1995.

Daintith, John. *A Dictionary of Physics.* New York, NY: Oxford University Press, 2010.

De Pree, Christopher. *Physics Made Simple.* New York, NY: Broadway Books, 2005.

Epstein, Lewis Carroll. *Thinking Physics: Understandable Practical Reality.* San Francisco, CA: Insight Press, 2009.

Glencoe McGraw-Hill. *Introduction to Physical Science.* Blacklick, OH: Glencoe/McGraw-Hill, 2007.

Heilbron, John L. *The Oxford Guide to the History of Physics and Astronomy.* New York, NY: Oxford University Press, 2005.

Holzner, Steve. *Physics Essentials For Dummies.* Hoboken, NJ: For Dummies, 2010.

Jargodzk, Christopher, and Potter, Franklin. *Mad About Physics: Braintwisters, Paradoxes, and Curiosities.* Hoboken, NJ: Wiley, 2000.

Lehrman, Robert L. *E-Z Physics.* Hauppauge, NY: Barron's Educational, 2009.

Lloyd, Sarah. *Physics: IGCSE Revision Guide.* New York, NY: Oxford University Press, 2009.

Suplee, Curt. *Physics in the 20th Century.* New York, NY: Harry N. Abrams, 2002.

Taylor, Charles (ed). *The Kingfisher Science Encyclopedia,* Boston, MA: Kingfisher Books, 2006.

Walker, Jearl. *The Flying Circus of Physics.* Hoboken, NJ: Wiley, 2006.

Watts, Lisa et al. *The Most Explosive Science Book in the Universe... by the Brainwaves.* New York, NY: DK Publishing, 2009.

Zitzewitz, Paul W. *Physics Principles and Problems.* Columbus, OH: McGraw-Hill, 2005.

Books – Light and Sound

Berg, Richard E. *Physics of Sound.* Upper Saddle River, NJ: Benjamin Cummings, 2004.

Cobb, Allan B. *Light and Optics (Science).* New York, NY: Rosen Publishing Group, 2000.

Cobb, Vicki et al. *Light Action! Amazing Experiments with Optics.* Bellingham, WA: SPIE Publications, 2005.

Gardner, Robert. *Experiments with Light and Mirrors.* Berkeley Heights, NJ: Enslow Publishers, 2006.

Parker, Barry. *Good Vibrations: The Physics of Music.* Baltimore, MD: The Johns Hopkins University Press, 2009.

Taylor, Barbara. *Light, Color & Art Activities.* New York, NY: Crabtree Publishing Company, 2002.

Tocci, Salvatore. *Experiments With Light.* Danbury CT: Children's Press, 2002.

Waldman, Gary. *Introduction to Light: The Physics of Light, Vision, and Color.* Mineola, NY: Dover Publications, 2002.

Web Sites

Marvellous machines
www.galaxy.net/~k12/machines/index.shtml
Experiments about simple machines.

How Stuff Works – Physical Science
http://science.howstuffworks.com/physical-science-channel.htm
Topics on all aspects of physics.

PhysLink.com
www.physlink.com/SiteInfo/Index.cfm
Physics and astronomy education, research, and reference.

PhysicsCentral
www.physicscentral.com/about/index.cfm
Education site of the American Physical Society.

Physics 2000
www.colorado.edu/physics/2000/index.pl
An interactive journey through modern physics.

The Why Files
http://whyfiles.org/
The science behind the news.